THE ISLANDS SERIES

MINORCA

THE ISLANDS SERIES

†Achill
†The Åland Islands
†Alderney
†The Aran Islands
†The Isle of Arran
†The Island of Bute
*Canary Islands: Fuerteventura
*Cape Breton Island
*Corsica
*Cyprus
*Dominica
*The Falkland Islands
†Gotland
*Grand Bahama
†Harris and Lewis
†The Isle of Mull
†Lundy
†The Maltese Islands
*Mauritius
† Orkney
*Puerto Rico
*Rhodes
*The Ryukyu Islands
†St Kilda and Other Hebridean
  Islands

*Sardinia
†The Scilly Isles
*The Seychelles
†Shetland
*Singapore
†Skye
*The Solomon Islands
*Tasmania
†Uists and Barra
*Vancouver Island

in preparation
Bermuda
Crete
Fiji
Greenland
Guadeloupe
Guernsey
St Helena
Tobago
Valentia

* Published in the United States by Stackpole
† Published in the United States by David & Charles Inc
  The series is distributed in Australia by Wren Publishing Pty Ltd, Melbourne

MINORCA

by *DAVID WILSON TAYLOR*

DAVID & CHARLES : NEWTON ABBOT

STACKPOLE BOOKS : HARRISBURG

This edition first published in 1975
in Great Britain by
David & Charles (Holdings) Limited Newton Abbot Devon
in the United States in 1975 by
Stackpole Books Harrisburg Pa

ISBN 0 7153 6787 0 (*Great Britain*)
ISBN 0 8117 1032 7 (*United States*)

© DAVID WILSON TAYLOR 1975

*Set in eleven on thirteen point Baskerville
and printed in Great Britain
by Latimer Trend & Company Ltd*

CONTENTS

LIST OF ILLUSTRATIONS

7

LIST OF ILLUSTRATIONS

To Tess and our family,
lovers of
the 'Summer Island'

Map of Minorca

1 THE SUMMER ISLAND

MINORCA, second largest of the Balearic Islands, and the most easterly part of Spain, has an individuality and history that set it apart from other members of the group, yet no complete account of it has been written in English for over two hundred years.

The key to its character lies in its deep and sheltered harbour, Port Mahón, one of the finest in Europe, which brought it into contact with many of the ancient Mediterranean civilisations, awakening Minorcans to new ideas, and giving the island an international quality.

With its roots in the Eastern Mediterranean (its unique megalithic buildings have affinities with Egypt and Crete), it did not become Spanish until the fourteenth century. In the eighteenth and early nineteenth centuries—again because of its port— Britain, France and America formed strong links with the island, from which Minorcans once again experienced new ways of life.

Today, for other reasons, Minorca is still an international island. Each year an increasing number of tourists from Europe, America, South Africa and the Antipodes come to enjoy its sunshine and its 120 superb beaches, at some of which one can still be alone. Apart from the regular mail steamer, the port is now largely given over to watersports, and occasional cruise ships. The island is one of unusual charm, and remains unsophisticated and free from the tensions of modern life.

La isla blanca y azul (the white and blue island) Minorcans like to call it, referring to its trim white houses and turquoise sea. The contrasts of light and colour in sea, land and sky—at times as vivid and dazzling as a stage-set—captivate artists, and can induce a sense of complete relaxation, even of unreality. Silences can be profound, broken only by the sound of distant waves lashing against rocks, or of a human voice carried on the wind.

In the seventeenth century, the owner of a merchantman sailing between Plymouth and Minorca so loved the island that he aptly renamed his ship *The Summer Island*.

Accommodation in hotel, apartment or villa is of a high standard, and recreations include sailing, swimming, tennis, golf and riding. There is a local flying club. Minorcans greet visitors as friends, as if flattered they have come, for they are not dependent on tourism for a living. Those making a longer stay have opportunities of joining in their many cultural activities, particularly in art and music.

The flight by jet aircraft from London or other northern European capitals takes only two hours, from New York via Madrid and Barcelona about eight. The air-traveller has his first glimpse of Minorca as he crosses the island's frontier of high cliffs in the west. The brown land below at first seems flat and bare; but presently great tracts of forest appear, both inland and towards the coasts. As the plane loses height he will see small scattered townships and villages, all intensely white, spread round sandy inlets, and the island's network of dry-stone walls enclosing tiny fields. He may just catch sight of the deep port before touching down at Mahón International Airport.

As an alternative, the night packet steamer from Barcelona covers the 140 miles in eleven hours. One's car will be skilfully hoisted aboard in a net, like a head of livestock. Rising at dawn, one can assume the role of discoverer. The first part of the island to appear on the horizon may be the isolated cone of Monte Toro, its highest point—a sailors' landmark since the time of the Phoenicians—which, to quote an old text, 'may be discovered by Sea, in clear Weather, at twelve or fourteen leagues' Distance'. Sailing off the north coast, one has fine views of some of the island's majestic cliffs, and the headlands (each with its lighthouse) of Cavalleria and Favaritx. The final progress up Port Mahón, to the capital town of Mahón at its head, carries the traveller back in time, and ends in a dramatic and fitting land-fall.

SITUATION

Minorca (Spanish spelling, Menorca) is situated in the Western Mediterranean at latitude 39° 52′ North and longitude 4° 13′ East, 224km (140 miles) south-east of Barcelona. It is the farthest east of the Balearic group of islands, of which the others are Majorca, Ibiza and the smaller Cabrera and Formentera.

Minorca's nearest and largest neighbour, Majorca, lies slightly to the south-west, the two islands being only 29km (18 miles) apart at their nearest points. Ibiza lies 225km (144 miles) to the south-west. The Bay of Alcudia in northern Majorca, with its background of jagged mountains, can be clearly seen from most points along the south coast of Minorca, often silhouetted by flaming sunsets. It was no doubt this proximity that induced an Englishwoman to swim from one to the other in 1971. The channel between Majorca and Minorca is only about 100m deep, but Minorca's wilder northern coast is near the edge of a submarine sill or precipice, where the sea-bed plunges to 2,400m (8,000ft).

Minorca's position in the Mediterranean has influenced its history since ancient times. Within a radius of 300km (about 200 miles) lie peninsular Spain, the great sea-ports of the south of France, Corsica and Sardinia, Algeria and North Africa. It was thus accessible to early mariners from all directions, and Port Mahón became a regular port of call on their trade routes. Later, in the great days of the sail, it became of strategic importance to Britain and France as well as to the future of America, and was occupied by Britain for a total of seventy-one years between 1708 and 1802.

Minorca may be classed as one of the smaller Mediterranean islands, as it is only 48·7km long (about 30 miles) and varies in width from 19·5km (12 miles) to 13km (8 miles). It has an area of 701·840sq km (270 square miles), and is of low relief.

13

Although not without hills its highest point is only 359·96m (1,175ft). It is only one-fifth the size of Majorca.

It is therefore ideal in size for the tourist. A larger island could be too urbanised, a smaller one confining and claustrophobic. In Minorca one can be out of sight and sound of the sea if one wishes, but it is never far away.

THE PEOPLE

Minorca has a population of about 52,000, out of which Mahón, the capital, together with its two suburbs of Villa Carlos and San Luis, account for one half. Ciudadela, its second main town, in the west, has a little over 12,000 inhabitants. The only other town of any size is the inland one of Alayor, with a population of about 5,500. The remainder is distributed among the small towns of Mercadal, Ferrerias, San Cristobal, Fornells and San Clemente, together with the rural areas.

We have a fairly clear picture of the population pattern and growth in the past, even in early times. The population in the last centuries BC has been estimated by L. P. Garcia at about 5,000. This is deduced from the numbers of young men from the island who were reported by classical authors as having been recruited as mercenary slingers for service abroad.

These early peoples lived mainly in the southern half of Minorca, and this pattern persists. The comparative absence of coastal towns was due to the desire to avoid the ravages of both wind and piracy. Even more striking were the effects—which still persist—of the administrative policy of the British in the eighteenth century, when in 1713 they transferred the capital from Ciudadela to Mahón. This led to a decline of Ciudadela, and Mahón increased its population, a preponderance it still retains.

Accurate records of population growth in the eighteenth century are a legacy of the British occupation. A census in 1723 gave the population (excluding priests and the garrison) as 16,082. By 1782 it was 26,281, and this upward trend has continued. Recent

14

increases due to foreign settlers are unlikely to influence materially an anticipated further slow growth. The present population density is only 72 persons per square kilometre, as compared with Malta's 1,000 per square kilometre. This low figure is combined with a high standard of living and industry.

The Minorcans

Present-day Minorcans are of varied ancestry, which has sometimes left recognisable features. A north European look, with fair or even red hair is sometimes seen, and bespeaks an English, Irish or Scottish strain deriving from the eighteenth century or the Napoleonic Wars. Today there are a small number of Anglo-Minorcan marriages, but by and large the islanders are of Catalan descent as a result of substantial immigration in the late thirteenth century.

Minorcans have pleasant manners and are courteous to strangers. They are both industrious and artistic in temperament, and have that innate dignity of the Spaniard which permeates all classes.

The majority of Minorcans have not been great travellers, and were often reluctant to serve in the army overseas. In 1820, when Spain was compulsorily recruiting single men to fight in the American colonies, there was a rush to marry. Unlike islanders in northern Europe, they have not—with a few notable exceptions—become great sailors or sea-captains. They nevertheless maintain that sturdy independence of islanders everywhere, and think of themselves as Minorcans first, and then Catalans.

The language

Among themselves Minorcans speak Minorquin, a dialect derived from the Catalan language of north-eastern Spain. This was brought to the island by thirteenth-century Catalan immigrants. As Minorquin is no longer taught in schools, where the teaching medium is Castilian Spanish, all Minorcans also speak Spanish.

English is now being taught in Minorcan schools, which gave rise to a recent notice in a shop window: 'English Spoken in the Afternoon' (that is, when the child is home from school). Minorcans encourage visitors to talk Spanish, and may tactfully correct them with a disarming smile. With the increase in tourism, English is being increasingly spoken.

In spite of the smallness of the island, local accents persist in various parts. Owing to previous isolation, the Minorquin dialect has preserved many archaic Catalan words, and modified others. It adopted some Latin inflections from priests, Arabic words from the Moors, and French and English words from the times of the French and British occupations.

A survey made sixty years ago showed about a hundred English words still in use, many concerned with drink, carpentry and games. The last include *marbols* (marbles), the game introduced by British children in the eighteenth century, and still played. Another is *winderes* (windows), referring to the English type of sash window seen everywhere in the town of Mahón today.

The following are further examples: stirrup, mug, punch, gin, boy, turnscrew, *saydbor* (sideboard), pudding, kettle, haversack, pork, jacket, 'even all', and *beriks* (barracks).

SUN AND STORM

Minorca has a 'mediterranean type' climate, characterised by winter rainfall and summer drought, mild winters and hot summers. It has the additional features of all island climates, winds and passing showers. The monthly temperatures show a maximum average of 24·5°C (about 80°F) in August, and a minimum of 10·1°C (50°F) in January. Humidity can be high in August, but is frequently tempered by a breeze.

The mean annual rainfall is 508–762mm (20–30in). In the last two weeks of January the weather can be mild enough to have breakfast on one's patio; while summer, beginning at the end of May, can extend right through the 'little summer of St Martin' to the end of November.

Climatic Table

AVERAGE MONTHLY TEMPERATURES (CENTIGRADE)

January	10·1°	July	24·2°
February	10·3°	August	24·5°
March	12·2°	September	22·6°
April	14·3°	October	18·4°
May	17·6°	November	14·4°
June	21·4°	December	11·7°

Mean annual rainfall	508–762mm
Average humidity	70 per cent

Minorcans describe six different winds, suggesting a certain preoccupation with the subject. A north wind, the *tramontana*, can reach gale force, and is commonest in winter, coming across the Alps from Russia. It can be icily cold, and often brings rain. Next in frequency is the *llebeig* (south-west) which is mild. The other three most important are the *llevante* from the east, the *mistral* from the north-west (both formerly feared by mariners), and the *xaloc* (sirocco) from Syria, which is soft and languid.

Minorcan seasons

Minorcan seasons start with the briefest spring in March and April, and day temperatures between 12·2°C and 14·3°C. The early visitor will find the landscape unexpectedly green, the air clear and stimulating. Friesian cattle graze in fields yellow with the Bermuda buttercup. Sheep and young lambs abound, and gorse decks the downs. There are many of the English early summer flowers: narcissi, orchids, clematis, gladioli and lupins —even a rare wild peony.

A long dry summer follows, lasting from May until the end of October. July and August are the hottest months, when the landscape becomes parched and brown. Harvest comes in May and June.

October and November bring a brief autumn. This is delightful walking weather with temperatures still around 18·4°C. The farmer is now ploughing and sowing his land. The purple heath is in bloom.

Winter lasts from December till February, with average day temperatures between 11·7°C and 10·3°C. This is the rainy season and consequently the season of growth. The landscape becomes green again.

The climate does not appear to have changed much over the last two hundred years. Dr George Cleghorn, a young Edinburgh physician who went to Minorca in 1743 as a naval surgeon to the British garrison, has left these detailed meteorological readings from 1743 to 1749:

> The air is more pure and clear than in Britain, being seldom darkened by thick fogs. The summers are dry, clear, calm and excessively hot; the autumns moist, warm and unequal; at one time perfectly serene, at another cloudy and tempestuous.
>
> During the winter, storms though sometimes violent, the weather returns to its usual serenity. The spring is always variable, but bears a stronger resemblance to the winter than the summer season.
>
> In the compass of a year, the mercury seldom rises above 80°F, nor falls below the 48th degree. As autumn draws near, whirlwinds and thunder are frequent. In the nights lightning and meteors . . . Waterspouts are often seen, and break upon the shore.

No meteors have been seen in recent years, but occasional waterspouts have been observed. To daunt the timid traveller further, a rare snowstorm lasted for four days in 1788, and there has been a brief fall about every ten years since. The last occurred on the morning of 4 December 1973, preceded by an icy *tramontana*, and lasted half an hour. The press reported snow-balling by children in Mahón.

2 MINORCA DISCOVERED

A LL islands invite discovery, but some yield their secrets more readily than others. For its size Minorca offers an unusual variety of scenery and interest, and its many facets have to be sought out and savoured. On a brief summer visit, one may get the impression of just one more 'island in the sun'; yet a stay of several months, with leisure to explore, will still leave much undiscovered.

This diversity in scenery stems from the island's uniquely hybrid origin, which has influenced its population pattern from the earliest times. Minorca bears little resemblance to its nearest neighbour, Majorca, and its axis lying east to west (opposite to that of the other Balearics) gives a hint of oddity. One soon discovers the marked contrasts between the island's northern and southern parts, of which one writer, Professor E. M. Gilbert, has remarked that 'the north [of Minorca] is more Catalan than Balearic in relief and structure'. These peculiarities derive from its unique beginnings.

BIRTH OF AN ISLAND

Geologists believe that Minorca's northern part is no less than the remaining fragment of a lost continent, which extended in the Palaeozoic era (570 to 225 million years ago) from Corsica in the east, to the coast of Catalonia (in Spain) in the west and was joined to continental Europe in the north. Its southern half, however, is of quite different and later origin, being—like Majorca and Ibiza—the tip of a submerged mountain ridge (the

19

Betic Cordillera) that extends eastwards from the mainland of Spain at Alicante.

The northern part of Minorca is the oldest piece of land in the whole of the Balearics, and could be likened to the remains of a second Atlantis sunk beneath the seas. The union of its two parts to form the present island occurred in the late Cretaceous period (136 to 65 million years ago), and was brought about by a pro-

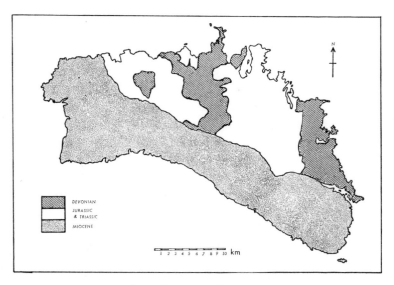

DEVONIAN
JURASSIC
& TRIASSIC
MIOCENE

1 2 3 4 5 6 7 8 9 10 km

Geological map of Minorca

cess of overlaying and folding, as a peripheral manifestation of the vast upheaval that gave rise to the Alps. Where at one point this fusion failed to take place, a great fault occurred, and the deep inlet of Port Mahón was born.

The boundary-line between the two different geological zones roughly bisects the island from east to west, extending from Mahón in the east, through the small inland towns of Mercadal and Ferrerias, then turning north just short of the western port of Ciudadela to a point below Algaiarens.

The oldest Primary sediments in Minorca were laid down in

the Silurian period (about 400 million years ago), and have been found at Mesquida and Fornells; but the matrix of the northern part of the island consists mainly of Primary Old Red Sandstone (Devonian), which occurs nowhere else in the Balearics. This is about 350 million years old, and its warm colour is quickly recognised as one travels across the island. The geological picture in the north is, however, complex and heterogeneous, as the Devonian strata have been much overlaid by younger rocks of the Secondary Triassic and Jurassic periods, usually of limestone. These areas often present a bleak and stark appearance, as at the Cap de Favaritx lighthouse, where one can imagine oneself on a lifeless planet. More pleasing to the eye, there are also in the north still younger Cretacean overlays, which have left us the great dunes and pink sands of Son Saura, and the almost ringed beach at Arenal d'en Castell.

If one wishes to relax in the sun, and day-dream on the tip of the lost continent, this can most easily be done on the large tract of land to the north-east of the capital town of Mahón, including the attractive beach at Cala Mesquida, and northwards to the fishing village of Es Grau and the islet of Colom. Two other such areas are the fishing village of Fornells, and the beaches of Binimel-lá.

The geological structure of the southern part of Minorca is entirely of the Tertian (Miocene) epoch (between 26 and 7 million years ago).

A falling away of the waters in the Pliocene epoch (Tertiary) sometime between 7 and 1·5 million years ago completed Minorca's birth. From fossils we learn that its early inhabitants included squirrels and giant tortoises, the former indicating that there were forests early in its history. The tortoises were peculiar to Minorca—a conundrum for zoologists. Minorca is the most senior of the Balearic Isles, having been isolated first. Majorca and Ibiza did not achieve island status till much later.

VEGETATION

Minorca's earlier reputation as a 'bleak and sterile island' is un-justified. In spring and autumn the beauty of innumerable wild flowers on roadside, field and even beach are a constant pleasure. Over 1,000 botanical land specimens have been identified.

Though less wooded than formerly, some 15 per cent of the island's surface is covered by forest, the most extensive being between the *playas* (beaches) of Santa Galdana and Macarella in the south, and Arenal d'en Castell, Son Saura and La Vall in the north. There are also extensive woods in the vicinity of the towns of Alayor and Mercadal.

Commonest is the Aleppo pine (*Pinus halepensis*), which, unlike the Mediterranean maritime pine, has slender, bright green spines and silver-grey twigs and branches: a colourful tree with its reddish-brown cones. When growing, as it often does, almost to the water's edge, its branches provide a pleasing framework for vistas of turquoise seas. Inland one finds the majestic and shady umbrella pine. Beneath the pines and among the ever-present rocks of limestone flourish a profusion of lesser evergreen shrubs and trees: the tenacious mastic tree (*Pistacia lentiscus*) with its red clustered flowers, the evergreen holly oak (*Quercus cocci-fera*), the sweet-scented myrtle (*Myrtus communis*) with its white flowers, and the Phoenician juniper (*Juniperis phoenicea*) with dark-red berries. From the crevices of rocks grow wild olive and fig trees. Many trees bend to the south at the behest of the *tramontana*; the main trunks of olive trees are often almost hori-zontal.

In October and early November the forests are waist-deep in purple heath, giving a distinctively Scottish appearance to the landscape, as at Macaret (near Arenal d'en Castell). One treads softly on beaten woodland paths carpeted by the pale mauve merendera (*Merendera montana*), a flower similar to an autumn crocus, but almost stemless and without leaf, its flower protrud-ing direct from the hard ground. In the same months one comes upon a tiny white narcissus—the autumn narcissus (*Narcissus serotinus*) in wood and hedgerow.

Once Minorca had more forests, and Armstrong, the author of this book's predecessor, writing in 1752, deplores the depredations of Minorcans themselves. He admits the British did the same, and confesses vividly: 'When the north Winds blow, we lay in our Wood very freely, and regale ourselves Indoors.'

PORT MAHÓN

As one approaches Port Mahón by sea, the modern naval station on Cap Mola lies to starboard, and on one's left is the spot where the formidable Fort St Philip once stood; scarcely a vestige remains.

At its entrance, Port Mahón is only 225m wide (250yd), with a depth of 8 fathoms; but this widens to a maximum of 900m (1,000yd) and deepens to 16 fathoms. It is 5·4km (6,000yd) long. It is thus almost landlocked, and its popularity with sailing ships as a refuge from Mediterranean storms is readily understood; for the *tramontana* is no respecter of persons, and the almost tideless sea is quickly whipped to fury. The only trouble appears to have been in leaving when the wind fell, or when it was blowing onshore. In the sixteenth century the famous Venetian Admiral Andrea Doria expressed this succinctly in the following couplet:

> Junio, Julio, Agosto y Puerto Mahón
> Los mejores puertos del Mediterráneo son.
> (June, July, August and Port Mahón
> Are the best ports in the Mediterranean.)

Entering the port one passes several islets. The first is New Quarantine Island, also known as Lazareto, which formed a peninsula until 1900. It is hardly 'new'; its high surrounding walls were built to prevent escape of infection! It has a unique circular chapel with an altar in its centre, and small barred cells for the sick around the periphery. The parson took no chances.

The small seaport of Villa Carlos on the left, around the bay of

Cala Fons, and formerly known as Georgetown, was built by the British shortly after 1763. Almost opposite it, in mid-stream, lies the Isla Plana or Old Quarantine Island, once an American naval base. The third islet, round which early-morning water-skiers skim, has an even more interesting history. The Isla del Rey, or King's Island, has three main claims to interest. A mosaic floor of its former Roman villa can be seen in Mahón's museum; King Alphonso III of Aragon landed on it in 1287, when Minorca first became Spanish; and it was later the site of the British hospital in the eighteenth century, when the troops christened it 'Bloody Island'.

On the hillside to the left stands the red Georgian villa of El Fonduco (now an hotel), which was Admiral Collingwood's residence towards the end of the Napoleonic Wars. On the opposite side of the port, high on its hillside and surrounded by yellow gorse, is the still more famous and noble villa of San Antonio or 'Golden Farm'. It commands a magnificent view of the whole port, and it was here that Nelson stayed on one of his visits to Port Mahón. Next comes the inlet of Cala Figuera on the left, known in the eighteenth century as 'English Cove'. It was the watering-place of the British Navy.

Soon, the capital town of Mahón comes into view; perched high on a cliff above the quay, the church of Santa Maria dominating the skyline. Dazzlingly white, Mahón has a typically Mediterranean aspect, though closer acquaintance reveals many familiar British traits.

THE ISLAND'S FACE

The southern half of the island consists of a low, undulating plateau varying in height from 45m (150ft) to 105m (350ft), broken by deep gorges or *barrancas*, which run north to south towards the sea.

In the absence of rivers, these canyons are a special feature of the island. They usually contain a sizeable stream, which may be seasonal, and is often dammed by farmers for irrigation.

Contours at intervals of 50 metres

Relief map of Minorca

They contain orchards and richly productive farmlands, and their vegetation is often sub-tropical: palm trees, lemon and orange trees, peaches and pomegranates and vines. They include some of the most beautiful and secluded parts of the island. The protecting sides of the *barrancas* are steep—in places precipitous—a tangle of mastic tree and juniper.

The hills

The central backbone of the island is pleasingly hilly. Monte Toro, 359·96m (1,207ft), Minorca's highest point, rises in comparative isolation near the centre of the island, with the white village of Mercadal at its foot. Seen from all directions, it crouches like a benign mother-figure over its domain. An excellent road leads to its summit, from which there is a panoramic view of the whole island. It is crowned by the seventeenth-century Renaissance church of the Virgin of Monte Toro, recently restored, and its beauty and peace make it worthy of a visit. A tall monument depicting Christ with outstretched arms is in curious juxtaposition to a giant radio and television relay aerial, for this is a radio and television 'boosting station'. There is also a medieval defence tower.

The road connecting the town of Alayor with Ferrerias via San Cristobal passes through delightful ravines and valleys, and to the west and north of Mercadal there are scores of small discontinuous summits, rising in a wholly disordered manner, with rather the appearance of a choppy sea. The lower slopes and valleys alternate between farmlands and pine forest. The chief of these lesser hills are S'Enclusa (274m) and Santa Agueda (264m). S'Enclusa rises just west of the town of Ferrerias, and is easily identified by installations of the American base on its summit: a relay station in the worldwide American military communications network. Santa Agueda has a long history. It also rises to the north of Ferrerias, and is reached by a secondary road a few miles to the west of that town. The climb is made by a Roman road, which is in a good state of preservation, and its precipitous summit is surrounded by the remains of a Roman fort with crumbling battlements. It was later converted by the Moors into a castle, now ruinous. The Moors put up a last defence here in 1287 against Alphonso III of Aragon.

The rural scene

The contrasts of colour and contour in the rural scene are enhanced by the bold outlines and dazzling whiteness of its farmhouses. The soil is a copper brown, and by moonlight the farmhouses look as white as snow. Their position on elevated sites often indicates their considerable age, and a preoccupation with the possibility of a raid by pirates or Moors. Massive buttressed square towers which sometimes form part of the farmhouses indicate a similar fear in medieval times. The approach will be through a typical rustic wooden gate, along a rough road bordered by high dry-stone walls often of massive stones, and the house will be surrounded by a field of enormous prickly pears (Barbary fig)—believed to have been imported from America, and used for cattle fodder. Its fields, and even isolated stunted trees, will be surrounded by a network of similar walls, often built of massive stones. Widespread wall-building in the southern part of the island began in the early fourteenth century, and the walls are known as *tancas*. As well as preventing erosion of soil and giving protection from wind, they are helpful in retaining animals.

As one approaches a farm, lean dogs bark a friendly welcome. The front of the farmhouse faces south, and most of its shutters are kept permanently closed against sun and rain. It probably has a wide, deep covered patio with arches, which runs the whole length of the house. If large and old, the ground floor is given over to storage rooms, outdoor oven, stables and byre, with the living rooms in the upper floors. The intense whiteness may extend to the tiled roof. As contrast there may be vivid splashes of colour from a variety of geraniums in gaily painted pots. There will be no garden. In summer additional colour is provided by the vivid yellow splash of marrows ripening in the sun. A television mast completes the picture.

The south coast

The south coast does not contain a single town, but is a succession of idyllic beaches interspersed with majestic cliffs. There are about a dozen major *playas*, each widely different in character. Most are at present under tourist development—'urbanisation' is the ugly word used—and each year new hotels and villas appear, but building is being carried out with discretion and imagination. In addition are many smaller coves, more difficult to reach but well worth the adventure.

Proceeding westward along the south coast the first beach is Alcaufar, a narrow cleft with a hotel and residential chalets. It was here that the British landed in 1708 when they first conquered and occupied the island, and it was a disembarkation point for Spanish troops under the Duc de Crillon in the Franco-Spanish invasion of 1781.

Nearby is the tourist complex of S'Algar, boldly sited on a rocky stretch of coastline with no beach, but of great charm. Sloping down towards the sea, it has hotels, swimming pools, attractive villas, shops, restaurants, sports clubs and green lawns. The predominant flowers are pink and white oleanders and canna lilies.

Next along the coast are the *playas* of Punta Prima and Binibeca, reached through San Luis. The former has attractive hotels, some on the chalet system. Offshore lies the Isla de l'Aire, with a lighthouse. It was off this island that Admiral Byng's unsuccessful battle against the French in 1756 cost him his life. Zoologists visit the Isla de l'Aire to see the unique black lizards which are a subspecies indigenous to this island.

At Binibeca is a delightful beach, with a *bar-restaurante* in a stone boathouse on the rocks, which rightly claims that it is 'the only bar where one can drink with one's feet in the sea'. The name Binibeca is Arabic in origin, the prefix 'Bini' meaning 'belonging to the sons of'. A little further along the coast is a tourists' summer fishing village built in Catalan style, dazzlingly white, with narrow alleys and gay balconies. It has a slipway for boats and facilities for swimming from the rocks.

Several small undeveloped beaches follow, like Binidali and Canutells; their names are also of Arab origin. They are best approached through the village of San Clemente. The swimmer will find seclusion and limpid clear water. Biniasfua is a perfect spot for deep water swimming from the rocks.

Two widely contrasting inlets of the sea follow, Cales Coves and Cala'n Porter (also occasionally spelt Cala en Porter). They adjoin each other, separated only by spectacular cliffs, and resemble small Norwegian fjords. In terms of human occupation they are nearly four thousand years apart. Cales Coves is the site of the largest group of cave dwellings on the island. Cala'n Porter is at present the island's most complete tourist and residential township, with a magnificent beach, and is completely equipped for either holidays or permanent living. A hotel, restaurants, and several shops and supermarkets are concentrated in a pleasant commercial area on high ground above the beach, and there are widely scattered residential zones with some 700 villas. Pioneer residents are mostly concentrated near the commercial zone, but later arrivals have either chosen more elevated sites commanding wide sea-views, or faced inland to enjoy restful landscapes; while the 'cliff-hangers' have built villas not suitable for sleep-walkers. Discreetly tucked away in one corner is the discothèque of Cova d'en Xoroi—in a vast cave in the cliffs.

Upstream for 5km (3 miles) from the beach stretches a *barranca* with an attractive orchard of oranges, lemons, apricots and vines. A pathway leading alongside it makes a pleasant walk.

Cala'n Porter is the only development to have a regular and frequent bus service to Mahón. It has electricity and a chlorinated water supply, and as one of the few 'colonies' which come directly under the administration of its nearest municipality at Alayor, is on the way to becoming the first ever 'new town' on Minorca's south coast.

There follows along the south coast a chain of major beaches unrivalled in Europe for beauty. The first is the 3km stretch of white sands which include the *playas* of Son Bou and San Jaime. The easiest approach is by the splendid new road just west of Alayor, taking one directly on to the beach by a spectacular tunnel through the rocky hillside behind it.

High up on this hillside and facing the sea are prehistoric cave dwellings and defensive walls, evidence of its early occupation. The old name for Son Bou was an Arab one: Ses Canessies, meaning 'Christian church', but its meaning appears to have been forgotten for many centuries, as it was not until 1951 that the ruins of a fifth-century Byzantine basilica were excavated right by the water's edge. Where Son Bou merges into San Jaime, the hillside is covered in pinewoods, with white villas built among the trees. One may return to the main road by the San Jaime highway.

The next group are the twin *playas* of Santo Tomas and Santo Adeodato, which are a continuation of the two beaches just described, separated from them by a low headland. They are best approached via the island's central road, turning off at the village of San Cristobal. These attractive beaches have pinewoods to the water's edge, a number of hotels, and a sports centre.

Cala Santa Galdana, often called the 'Queen of the Playas', is the centrepiece of the last group of beaches on the south coast. It is a half-circle of white sands and crystal-clear emerald water, sheltered from the north by rugged cliffs clad in pine, and embraced by noble headlands. Until a few years ago it was a solitary place, but now has several large hotels and is crowded in summer. Some Minorcans are not too happy about what they have done, and think the 'Queen' should abrogate her title.

The largest permanent stream on the island enters the sea at Galdana, after traversing its greatest *barranca*—the Barranca of Algendar. The Moors knew and used the shelter of Santa Galdana, which they named Guad-al-Anna, this name being later corrupted in Christian times to its present one, although there is no saint of that name.

Galdana's attendant beaches are Cala Mitjana and Trebaluger to the east, and Macarella and Macarelleta farther west. These are best reached on foot through the pinewoods which here reach to the edge of the cliffs. Trebaluger is the least accessible, and has a Robinson Crusoe quality, with a two-roomed cave beside its pink sands, and a brook of fresh water running past one's 'door'. The scene seems unchanged since antiquity.

Cala Mitjana, incredibly blue and scintillating, to which one clambers down through rocks and pine, is small and intimate. Beyond it lies a larger arm to which one can swim. The twin *calas* of Macarella and Macarelleta are so close that one can also swim from one to the other, or traverse the prehistoric rock steps in the intervening cliff. In medieval times these beaches were the favourite hide-outs of Barbary pirates raiding the island.

The western end

The western end of the island is less attractive than the south, and like the extreme east is rather flat and bare. Its main feature is the island's second town, Ciudadela, which is as strongly Spanish in architecture and character as Mahón is British. The one provides a pleasing contrast to the other.

Ciudadela has a modest harbour some 1,000m in length. There are several small beaches in the vicinity notably Santandria and Cala Blanca. Near the latter are the notable Caves of Parella, which have stalagmites and stalactites, and a small underground lake. The more distant beaches of Cala Turqueta, Arenal de Son Saura and Cala Bosch lie to the south. Cala Turqueta is rated highly by many visitors, and still undeveloped.

THE CONTRASTING NORTH

In general the northern coastline is more indented and the cliff scenery more majestic and impressive than in the south. It receives the full blast of the *tramontana*, and in winter the spray can rise hundreds of feet in a white mist above distant headlands. The finest view in Minorca—or of it—is from the lighthouse at the tip of the long, finger-like promontory of Cap Cavalleria, looking south across the island. This is the island's most northerly point. In the immediate foreground is a little bay that is the forgotten Phoenician and Roman port of Sanitja, and beyond it an expanse of sea and cliff scenery on both sides, with a background of the whole of the island's hills, panoramic and breathtaking.

Fornells

With the exception of the fishing village of Fornells in the bay of the same name, the north coast, like the south, has no township. Fornells has been a fixed centre of population for centuries on account of its port, which is almost as long as Port Mahón and wider. The Bay of Fornells (pronounced 'Forneys') is 5km long and 2km wide, but is shallower than Port Mahón, and difficult to navigate. The village is situated near its mouth on the west bank of the bay. Apart from a row of palm trees on the quay, it is reminiscent of Cornwall, with its fishing craft and lobster creels, and attracts artists and lovers of boats.

On the headland beyond the village stood the ancient castle of Fornells, now in ruins. In 1741 it was a square fort with four bastions and curtain walls, large enough inside to have houses bordering on a square, to accommodate a small garrison with stores and ammunition. Fornells was a secondary invasion port in the first British expedition against Minorca in 1708.

In the bay is the Illa de Ses Sargantanes ('Lizard Island'), which like the isle of Aire in the south, has a subspecies of reptile peculiar to it.

Beaches and lakes

The north has several magnificent beaches, and many more tiny ones which have to be sought out. The major ones include Binimel-Lá, lying to the west of Fornells, and Arenal de Son Saura and Arenal d'en Castell to the east. All of these are backed by sand-dunes. Cala Tirant and Binimel-lá have small lagoons. They are all at present under tourist development, and are approached by good roads.

Page 33 View of Port Mahón and the city from the air

Page 34 Mahón, the capital of the island: (*above*) in the early morning sun; (*below*) view from the quay

Among unusual beaches—both best approached from Ciudadela—are Cala Morell and Algaiarens. Algaiarens is a twin beach approached through a fertile pine-clad valley known as La Vall, and also has a lagoon.

The northern coast has two further unique features. If one follows the sign-post marked Port Addaya on the road to Arenal d'en Castell, one is suddenly amid scenery of the Scottish western Highlands: a long narrow inlet of the sea like a sea loch sheltered by low hills on each side. In October or November these slopes will be covered by heather. Addaya is 3·5km long, with several islets and the small fishing hamlet of Na Macaret at its mouth. This idyllic and lonely spot was the main disembarkation point of the last British expedition against the island in 1798, under General Sir Charles Stuart.

The second is the island's least-known feature: its beautiful lake, Albufera. More than a mile long, it lies hidden by low hills to the west of the fishing village of Es Grau, only 6·8km from Port Mahón. The pleasant lagoon which adjoins the road on approaching the village is the lake's outlet by means of a sandbar on the nearby beach. The lake has an islet, and a background of hills to the west.

Albufera abounds in wild duck and other game. In the eighteenth century it was a favourite goal for the shooting and fishing expeditions of the British garrison, and we read of it as 'abounding in red mullets, and harbouring in winter an amazing variety of wild fowl'. It is now a nature reserve and bird sanctuary. Of his excursions to Albufera Armstrong wrote: 'one undergoes more hardship and fatigue in a day's shooting, which we call a diversion, than in three weeks of the strictest duty an officer is put to'.

3   PREHISTORIC MINORCA

THE classical author Diodoro of Sicily, writing in the first century AD, quotes Timeo as saying about 350 BC: 'Off the coasts of Spain are groups of islands the Greeks call "Gymnesias", because the inhabitants go about naked during the summer.' In Minorca they lived in caves in the cliffs and rocks, and because of their marauding habits have been likened to beachcombers. Recent carbon-14 dating has resulted in pushing back by nearly 2,000 years previous estimates of the arrival of these Neolithic men. There is now evidence of human presence as far back as about 4000 BC. When Homer was writing about 800 BC of the legendary adventures of Odysseus in the Western Mediterranean, Minorca had probably been inhabited for 2,000 years.

The detective story starts with the discovery in 1909 of the remains of *Myotragus balearicus*, an extinct Balearic mountain antelope, believed to have died out long before man's arrival on the island. In 1958 the American archaeologist W. Waldren, working in Majorca, made a large find of bones of this animal, which gave a carbon-14 date of 5184 BC (plus or minus eighty years), proving that the antelope had survived until a later date than previously supposed. The breakthrough came in 1962 when the Minorcan archaeologist Sr G. Florit Piedrabuena found in a cave (Cova Murada, at Algendar, near Ciudadela) horns of an antelope which had been trimmed to form a tool, with Neolithic globular pottery in the same stratum. This proved that man and *Myotragus* were contemporaries. Between then and 1965, he obtained further proof from five other Minorcan cave sites, which revealed similar coexisting material. In the follow-

36

ing year carbon dating of both human and animal material in both Minorca and Majorca gave a reading of 3984 BC (plus or minus 100 years). These facts taken together confirmed man's presence in Minorca in about 4000 BC.

BALEARIC CAVE CULTURE

These early Neolithic settlers are generally referred to as belonging to the 'Balearic Cave Culture', or the 'Pre-Talayot period', a term meaning a period prior to that of the talayots or 'towers' of

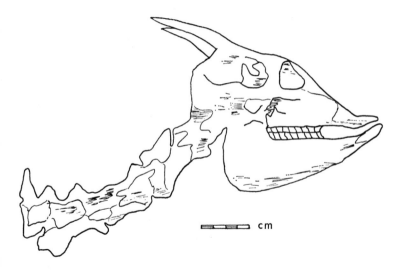

Myotragus Balearicus

Minorca. They probably came from the Spanish (Iberian) mainland, via Majorca, and must have been adventurous sailors in their frail skin or log boats. Possibly their first landfall was accidental as a result of storm or shipwreck. Perhaps they found a sheltered cove, a welcoming cave and fresh water in a wooded *barranca*, as they took their first steps inland. As the centuries passed, and others came, they formed communities and lived in groups in caves, both natural ones and others which they cut out of the soft limestone in the southern part of the island.

These can best be seen at Cales Coves—near Cala'n Porter—which is the largest group of caves in the Balearics. The precipitous cliffs of this Y-shaped cove are honeycombed with 145 man-made caves, tier above tier, the upper ones only accessible by tenuous footholds. Because of the oblique angle of the cove, it is quite hidden from the open sea. This choice of site showed considerable cunning; it enabled them to make a sudden sea raid, and quickly retire. If their lair was discovered, they evacuated their caves and climbed the cliffs by a secret pathway which still exists, retiring behind a cyclopean defence wall, from which they hurled stones down at the intruder.

The majority of these caves were probably originally communal burial chambers, but later became dwellings, and remained in occupation for 1,500 years. Many have a shaped doorway, usually raised, a vestibule, a large central room, and alcoves. Today a few are occupied in summer by weekend fishermen.

A second smaller but important cave group is at Cala Morell in the north-west of the island. Cave no 12 has a sculptured façade, and a central pillar in the interior, with a low dais and four adjoining rooms.

Little is known of the daily lives of these Neolithic men, but as new arrivals became more frequent, new ideas, techniques and knowledge were absorbed. Among these were the use of metals and processing of bronze, and as we shall presently see, the handling of large stones in building. As evidence of the first Minorcans' intelligence and achievements in medicine, Neolithic human skulls have been found in caves near Mercadal, which were surgically trephined during life; and around the neatly punched holes was a callus thickening of bone, giving evidence of a healing process. The patient survived.

Dates in prehistory can be only approximate, but it is thought that the Talayot period, which succeeded the Cave Culture, began about 1400 BC, and coincided roughly with the Bronze Age. The word 'talayot' is derived from the Arabic word *atalaya* (a tower), being the most typical and commonest megalithic building on the island of this period.

Professor Garcia, Director of the Institute of Prehistory at Barcelona University, has subdivided the Talayot period into three phases: Talayot I—1400 BC to 800 BC; Talayot II (coinciding with Phoenician and Greek influence)—800 BC to 500 BC; and Talayot III—500 BC to 200 BC. Taken together these extend to a period of 1,200 years, during which a comparatively small population raised some 1,600 buildings of gigantic proportions.

The other principal types of megalithic building found associated with the talayots in the ancient settlements are the 'Taula' (T-shaped monument) which is unique to Minorca, the 'naveta' (or boat grave), and the hypostyle court (a chamber of unknown use).

The technique of megalithic building was brought by a new kind of migration of people from the east, towards the middle of the second millennium BC, when it spread all over western Europe, including France, Ireland and Britain as far north as the Orkney Islands. They propagated the cult of chamber-tomb group burial, and inspired more than 50,000 megalithic buildings. It is believed to have been a migration of small groups, whom circumstances led at different times to seek a new life.

Today we might call them intellectuals or professional classes —engineers, architects, priests, craftsmen. Professor C. D. Darlington of Oxford University believes that they were possibly 'refugees of civil wars, exiled noblemen, and generals'.

Owing to the aura of mystery which surrounds these people, they are often simply referred to as 'the peoples of the seas'. It is

thought they may have sailed as passengers in Phoenician ships—
the Phoenicians were expert mariners—and that they may have
come from Egypt, Crete or the Aegean, leaving behind some of
their number in Malta, Sardinia, Corsica and Minorca.

Talayots

Talayots sometimes occur in two or threes as part of a prehistoric township, but are also found in isolation. They are vast
truncated cones of giant stones, as much as 10m high, with a
diameter of from 15m to 20m. Like the talayot at Trepucó just
outside Mahón, most appear to be quite solid. They are the only
megalithic buildings on the island of which similar ones exist on
Majorca, although the latter are much smaller, and of different
design. Comparisons have also been made with the giant
Nuragh towers of Sardinia, but these could be distant 'cousins'
only. Minorca has about 200 talayots, so that they were clearly
important.

While those on elevated sites, as at the ancient township of
Torre d'en Gaumés (near Son Bou, Alayor), were probably
watch or defence towers, some had a central chamber and could
have served a double purpose as the residence of a Bronze Age
chief. An excellent example of this is at Son Agusti Vell (on a
farm near San Cristobal) where a corridor leads to a central
chamber which has three pillars and a corbelled roof of large
stone slabs, with some original olive-wood beams, possibly 3,000
years old. Talayots show no evidence of a superstructure, though
they could have had one of wood and wattle. If this were so, the
chief's dwelling could have been on top, the lower chamber being
used for animals and stores, as is common practice today in old
Spanish farmhouses.

Taulas

Taulas (literally 'tables'), enigmatic symbols of a forgotten
religion and unique to the island, occupy a central and important position in the prehistoric settlements. There are no taulas
in Majorca, or anywhere else, so they could be called Minorca's

trademark. They are the oldest megaliths on the island, with the exception of the navetas, and out of a total of thirty taulas there are only seven still complete.

Each consists of a vertical monolith as high as 4·20m and 2·75m wide, with a horizontal capstone of massive proportions placed on top and widely overlapping its upper end. The front surface of the vertical stone and the upper surface of the horizontal one have been smoothly dressed with tools, while their opposite sides are rough and untouched virgin rock. The edges of the capstone are carefully squared and bevelled inwards, so that both stones together seem to make an extremely high table, with a central pedestal leg. The mason's greater attention to the capstone suggests a religious importance. The vertical monolith is maintained erect by being sunk in a groove in the bedrock of the site chosen, and the delicate balance of the capstone is sometimes aided by a shallow chiselled mortice on its under surface.

A taula is usually surrounded by a horseshoe-shaped *circulo* of massive stones, with remains of a lintelled opening, usually towards the south. This gives the impression of a sanctuary, thought to have been built some time after the taulas themselves. Good examples of these sanctuaries can be seen at the prehistoric town known as Torre d'en Gaumés (near Alayor), and at the taula and ancient village of Torralba d'en Salort (on the road between Cala'n Porter and Alayor). The largest taula is Trepucó on the outskirts of Mahón (approached by the street named Cos de Gracia), and has the dimensions already quoted. The engineering problem posed in raising and balancing these great masses of stone in primitive times baffles the imagination.

Near Torralba d'en Salort, an opportunity should be taken to visit at the adjoining farm the ancient great stepped well of Na Patarrá, dating from about 700 BC. The mouth of this well measures 7·50m by 5m; its 199 steps are in nine flights, together with a stone handrail, all hewn out of the rock. It resembles ancient Palestinian wells, and was probably used by the actual builders of the taula on the site.

Talatí de Dalt is another Bronze Age village (just off the

Mahón–Alayor main road) with a taula, talayots and hypostyle courts. This taula is unusual in having an extra smaller, oblique vertical monolith.

The absence of metal tool markings on the taula of Trepucó, Talatí, Son Catlar and one at Torre Llafuda suggest that they are the oldest—probably Neolithic. By contrast the taula at Sa Torreta, near Es Grau and one of the few situated on the north coast, was built about 1,000 years later. This indicates the extent of time during which megalithic building took place.

The question of whether taulas had a functional or religious purpose has been hotly disputed by amateur and professional archaeologists for two hundred years. John Armstrong's book *A History of the Island of Minorca* contains an engraving of a taula, which he refers to as a 'heathen monument'; he was convinced they were used for human sacrifices. This is no longer believed. Nor is much credence given to the theory that the taula was a centre post for a roof made of wood and reeds. A theory propounded by Waldemar Fenn in 1950 suggesting that they were some kind of astronomy computer has also failed to find many adherents.

It is now widely believed that they had a profound religious meaning, and the Spanish archaeologist J. Mascaró Pasarius suggested in 1967 that the taula was a stylised representation of a god-bull in which the horizontal capstone portrays the wide horns. Analogies are made with the bull cult in Minos in Crete. This theory has much to support it. Worship of the bull as the essence of strength and fertility was common at this period throughout the Eastern Mediterranean.

The driving force which impelled Minorcans—so small in numbers—to the gargantuan task of raising the taulas could only have been a religious one, based on instincts for survival and continuance of their race, strong in primitive man. These instincts in Minorcans were frequently challenged by famine from failure of crops, and by death from disease, so that we would expect them to take part in the then current rites associated with the fertility of soil and man. There is evidence of this in the phallic symbols found on amulets in the vicinity of taulas, and the remains of small horned animals (sheep and goats) commonly used in sacrifices in Malta and Minoan Crete.

A second, and equally powerful, motivation was the Minorcans' belief in an after-life, as suggested by their navetas (communal graves). Sceptics may mock at their hopes of immortality, but at least the work of their hands endures, apparently for all time. Too much stress should not be placed, however, on the cyclopean stones, which were but a fashion in building. In later ages the architects and craftsmen who raised Europe's medieval cathedrals were expressing a similar if more spiritually mature urge to build for the future, which is apparently inherent in man.

Navetas

Navetas are collective burial chambers built, above ground level, of cyclopean stones, situated at a distance from the centres of population. Their design is unique to the island; they were first called navetas in 1818 because their shape resembles an upturned boat. There are thirty-six on the island, the most notable being the Naveta des Tudons, which is stated by Professor Garcia to be the oldest roofed building on Spanish soil and possibly in Europe. It is sign-posted on the left of the Ferrerias–Ciudadela road, and is easily reached by car. This naveta is 14m long by 6·4m (maximum) wide and about 8m high, with an easily negotiated entrance at its 'blunt' end leading to two superimposed burial chambers. It is not known whether the upturned-boat shape is deliberate. It is probable that the shape is simply due to corbelling of the roof.

When the Naveta des Tudons was excavated in 1959 many of the original deposits were found to be undisturbed. In its main chamber, among hundreds of human bones, were perforated bone buttons and metal discs of the same type as those associated with the *Myotragus balearicus*. On female skeletons were found bronze bracelets still around the bones of the arms they had once adorned. The women had not been slow to admire the beauty of the new metal as well as its usefulness.

Hypostyle courts

Hypostyle courts (literally 'low-pillared chambers'), found in many of the ancient settlements we have been exploring, are dug-outs, half above and half below ground, lined and roofed by massive slabs of stone. The roof slabs seem to be placed at random, and are supported by low pillars, often of the Mediterranean type (that is, wide at the top and tapering downwards). The mechanics of building defy imagination. The fact that great labour was involved suggests they may have been places of assembly of chiefs or elders. An excellent example can be seen at Torre d'en Gaumés, and another alongside the talayot at Torralba d'en Salort, places already mentioned.

The walls of Son Catlar

Son Catlar is notable as the only prehistoric town still completely surrounded by a wall. It was described forty-seven years ago by Frederick Chamberlin in his book *The Balearics and their Peoples* as one of the most thrilling places on the island. Much of it still remains unexplored. It can be reached with a little effort from the country road leading from Ciudadela to Cala Turqueta, turning right at the fork to Son Saura, and stopping at the farm of Son Catlar.

Its massive defensive wall runs for 900m and encloses an area with a diameter of 160m. The state of preservation of the wall varies, but one section of it runs straight for 200m, and several former gateways can be detected. The Romans reoccupied the site later and added defensive turrets. Hidden by undergrowth in the centre of the enclosure is a sanctuary with a taula, with capstone fallen and broken. A large talayot has been built at each end, neither apparently with an opening, but one with an unusual cupola. Several impressive hypostyle courts have been built within the thickness of the massive surrounding walls, and the remains of many ordinary circular dwellings can be seen, many with vestiges of a hearth.

A pocket god

Many more ancient townships await excavation. An epoch-making discovery of a bronze figure of the Egyptian god Imhotep was made while clearing the sanctuary at Torre d'en Gaumés in 1974. Provisionally dated 650–550 BC, it is the first-ever Egyptian find in the Western Mediterranean.

Imhotep was architect, priest, physician and chief minister to the pharaoh of the Third Dynasty (2778–2723 BC), to whose all-round achievements posterity added others, finally deifying him. The delicately worked figure shows him in a seated position, reading a papyrus on his knees. On his ovoid head (an art style that helped in dating) he wears a skull-cap; his other dress is a breastplate with collar, knee-length striped skirt, over-apron, and sandals.

The statue could have been brought to the island by one of the early migrant exiles from the East. It is only 6in high, a pocket-sized god suitable for travelling.

DAILY LIFE IN EARLY MINORCA

The first Minorcans were a pastoral people, who grew wheat and barley, and tended their cattle, sheep, goats and pigs. (It is thought they may also have hunted the *Myotragus* (antelope) to extinction.) In the cooler seasons they probably wore skins. They built small boats, and indulged in coastal piracy when opportunity offered. But among their number were some with other skills. In addition to the metal workers, they had an élite of gifted constructional engineers, and we shall try to imagine their technique.

An outcrop of rock near the proposed site for building would be chosen, which it is thought may have been split by inserting a piece of wood in an existing crack, wetting it till it expanded. Alternatively they may have found that the growing trunk of a fig tree in an existing crack had produced a similar splitting. The slab would then be levered with poles on to rollers, and dragged over a prepared roadway by means of leather ropes to the proposed site of erection. There it was chipped by masons to the desired shape and size, dressed and polished.

In the case of a taula, enormous ramps of stones or sand would then be prepared, and the upright levered into a prepared hole. By the use of further ramps the tricky business of levering and pulling the capstone into position was undertaken.

It is difficult to estimate the man-hours for the whole operation from raw material to end product. The number of able-bodied young men on the island must have been limited. Perhaps the entire male population and some of the women took part. In the organisation of their society there may have been some kind of compulsory community service. This was not unknown in the feudal society of the Middle Ages, and has a parallel in military conscription in our own country.

Slingers for hire

One more activity of first Minorcans which outlasted their building achievements, and brought them renown throughout the then civilised world, was their skill with the sling. The Roman historian Timeo reports in the fourth century BC (Phase III of the Talayot period): 'the inhabitants of these isles were called the *Balears*, on account of their skill in throwing stones by means of slings'. The stone-strewn island provided unlimited ammunition. New arrivals on the island were frequently on the receiving end of an attack by the slingers, but usually ended up by enlisting them as mercenaries to help them fight their own battles elsewhere.

Minorcans reduced slinging to a fine art. Each man carried three slings of different sizes, and ammunition of polished stones was also graded. The thongs were of leather or plaited esparto grass. He carried one sling round his head, one at the shoulder, and one in his hand, selecting the most suitable for the range required, rather as a golfer would a club. His aim was said to be deadly, even at a hundred yards. Training in the art was begun in childhood—an early form of vocational training—and was undertaken by the mothers. A tall wooden post was set up, and food balanced on the top. The children had to knock it down with stones—otherwise they had no breakfast!

By a brilliant piece of research we know quite a lot about the physique of the slingers, and even what they looked like. In 1932 Dr Margaret Murray, the famous Egyptologist led a team of excavators from Cambridge University to Minorca, where they excavated the precincts of the taulas of Trepucó and Sa Torreta. There she unearthed numerous sling-stones and other objects dating from the first millennium BC, together with human bones of the same period. She submitted these to Dr John Cameron, a professor of anatomy, who reported a remarkable development of the upper end of the *humerus* (upper arm bone) and of the *scapula* (shoulder blade), indicating over-development of the shoulder-rotating muscles. Even more striking was an actual bowing of the shaft of the upper arm bone itself, as a result of constant rotation of the arm since childhood.

Professor Cameron has also written a pen picture of the physical appearance of a Minorcan slinger, as deduced from his bone structure, which was as follows:

His average height was only 5 feet $5\frac{1}{2}$ inches, a somewhat aquiline prominent nose, a rather prominent pointed chin. The relatively fine bones of the jaws indicated that they were accustomed to cooked food. The relatively short thigh bones exhibited a flattening of the articular surfaces due to constant squatting. Lest the overall impression be of the early Minorcan being extremely primitive, I may add that their cranial capacity—both children and adults—were up to that of modern European skulls, and in one case above it.

4 FORMATIVE INFLUENCES TO 1700

AS the Talayot culture waned, a succession of new peoples put in at the island's sheltered harbours for fresh food and water. Some, like the Phoenicians, returned to trade, while Greeks, less adventurous sailors, stayed to found small colonies. Any invaders, like the Carthaginians and Romans, were met by a hail of stones from the slingers.

Up to AD 1700 arrivals and departures were numerous—nine in all—and a chronological table is provided in an appendix to assist the reader. Emphasis is placed on the influence of four. The first three are the Romans, the Moors and the kings of Aragon, each of which ruled Minorca for about 500 years. The fourth is the little-known and brief stay of Samuel Pepys's navy at Port Mahón in the mid-seventeenth century, the ultimate consequences of which were to shape the island's future for the next hundred and fifty years.

PHOENICIANS, GREEKS AND CARTHAGINIANS

Between 1600 BC and 1200 BC biremes of Phoenician traders (galleys with square sails and two tiers of oars) were increasingly seen in Minorcan *calas*. These expert mariners were among the first to navigate by the stars, and came from Biblos, Tyre and Sidon on the Syrian coast. They put in at Minorca during voyages to Tarsis in the south of Iberia (Spain), where they owned land and zinc mines.

They set up trading-posts on the present sites of Port Mahón and at Ciudadela. Pliny in his *History* also tells us of a settlement at Sanisera (the modern Sanitja), a small and delightful inlet

48

with two sandy coves on the north coast near the Cavalleria lighthouse. The position of this port is interesting, for early mariners hugged coasts when they could, and this suggests an approach from the southern European coast. The Romans also used Sanitja, but all trace of its town and port have disappeared. It lies deserted save for an occasional fishing boat or swimmer.

The attention of Phoenician sailors was first drawn to Minorca by the many fires seen on it at night, on account of which they gave the island its first known name—Nura (fire). The fires could have been a method of signalling between elevated points, or simply heath fires during the dry hot summers caused by wind-blown embers from domestic hearths. The Phoenicians have left little to remind us of their presence. A few bronze objects and fragments of Phoenician coloured glass have been found in graves in the cliffs near Sanitja. They are said to have introduced to Minorcans the classical long tunic of the ancients, with its purple hem, and shown them how to extract the purple dye from the tiny molluscs (murax) still found on its shores.

Greek traders began to arrive about 500 BC, gradually supplanting the Phoenicians. The location of their settlements is not known, but they probably occupied many of the prehistoric sites. As one looks today at the island's numerous herds of Friesian cattle, it is interesting to note that the Greeks gave Minorca its second known name—Meloussa (Island of Cattle). The Greeks came from Phocis in the Eastern Mediterranean, probably by stages from Italy, Sardinia and Corsica. No Greek building of any kind has survived, although the megaliths were nearly a thousand years old when they came, and are still with us. A bronze statue of the goddess Minerva, and a bronze figure of an athlete, have, however, been found. In addition Greek pottery and amphorae have been raised from submarine wrecks around the island. Underwater sportsmen may try their luck.

The Carthaginians who followed a century later were the first to carry out a military expedition against Minorca. They occupied it as part of a wider conquest, which included not only the other Balearic Islands but North Africa and Iberia. They coined the name 'Baleares' for the island group, which has two possible derivations: from *Balein*—'to throw with a sling', or from 'Balari'—the name of a tribe in Sardinia.

They also made Minorcan slingers famous throughout the Mediterranean world by enlisting them as mercenaries in the First and Second Punic Wars. Minorcans became widely travelled, and some of the slingers probably accompanied Hannibal across the Alps with his elephants. At Trebia they opened the attack against the Roman armies. Classical writers tell us that when abroad the slingers preferred to receive their pay in the form of wine and women, instead of foreign currency in which they placed no trust. If any of the women were carried off by the enemy, they offered three or four captured men of rank in exchange for one of them.

The Carthaginians are said to have founded the present town of Ciudadela, calling it Jamma ('the West Town'), and Maghen, now Mahón. Although their relations with the islanders were at first good, there is a tradition that Minorcans rebelled against their masters in 252 BC, attacking them with knives and sinking many galleys in Port Mahón. The uprising was put down ruthlessly by Hannibal Barca.

Mago, the last commander of the Carthaginians, wintered at Port Mahón in 207 BC. From him the town took the name Port Magonis.

ROMAN MINORCA

When the Romans invaded Minorca on the decline of the Carthaginian power in 123 BC, they stayed for 550 years, so that their arrival was not so much another episode in the island's history as the beginning of an era. The initial reason for the occupation was to suppress the increasing tendency of Minorcans towards piracy, but also because of Port Mahón's strategic value. They gave the island yet one more name—Balearis Minor or Minorica.

The island's conqueror was Quintus Cecilius Metellus. He

Page 51   City Hall, Mahón, used by Governor Sir Richard Kane in the eighteenth
century, who presented the clock in its tower

Page 52 (*above*) Minorcan farmhouse in Algendar Canyon, a fertile ravine on the southern coast; (*below*) Cales Coves, the largest group of prehistoric cave dwellings on the island, dating from 1400 BC

was greeted with the usual shower of stones from the slingers, who rushed into the shallow water to attack the landing-parties as they disembarked. The Romans had taken the precaution of protecting vulnerable parts of their *triremes* with skins, and rammed them with their latest naval invention: a sharp under-water 'beak' in the prow of each galley. The slingers retired in-land to prepared positions in the talayots, with the Romans in pursuit. For the success of his campaign Quintus Metellus was rewarded in the 'honours list' of the Senate in Rome, with the style and title of 'Victor of the Balearics'.

The Romans brought order and settled government to Minorca, building many military roads, some of which can still be traced. They built a fort on the summit of the precipitous hill of Santa Agueda, and set up military strong-points throughout the island, which often made use of megalithic walls round the talayots and taulas. Examples of these can be seen at Torre Llafuda and especially at the ancient settlement at Son Catlar. During the occupation Port Magonum became of increasing importance, and was given municipal status with its own local government, and an additional title after a Roman emperor 'Flavium'. The Balearics were made a province of the Roman Empire, as they are of Spain today.

During the earlier years, Roman colonists were settled, and agriculture was improved. The type of plough they employed is still occasionally used. The islanders moved away from the old beliefs of the talayot period, and took part in a more sophisticated life. The Minorcan mercenary slingers continued to travel. They may have set foot in Britain long before the British did in Minorca, for the Romans used Spanish legions in Britain about the time of the battle of Mons Graupius. Minorcans could have been there.

Christianity in Minorca

An event of major importance in the life of the Minorcans during the Roman occupation was the coming of Christianity. It is not known precisely how and when it came. Paul twice states

D

his intention to visit Spain (Epistle to the Romans 15: 24, 28), in which case his ship would probably have called in at Port Mahón. Non-biblical sources—Clement of Rome and the Muratorian Canon (an Italian document written in Greek in the latter part of the second century AD)—indicate that Paul could have visited Spain in AD 63. The most certain date is, however, between AD 300 and 400, towards the end of the Roman era. The oldest Christian document referring to Minorca is dated AD 417, and was a letter from Bishop Severo of Minorca to the Christian world, a copy of which still exists in the Vatican.

The remains of four Palaeochristian basilicas have been discovered on the island during the last twenty-five years. The best known is at Son Bou on the south coast, and lies on the shore of a three-mile stretch of beach. It was discovered in 1951. By comparison with similar churches in North Africa, it is believed to date from the Byzantine period (the end of the fifth century AD), and it has a unique circular font carved out of a cyclopean block of limestone. A second basilica, approached by a narrow farm road at Fornas de Torelló, near Mahón, was discovered by a farmer who was clearing a field of stones as late as 1956. All that survives are its magnificent Roman mosaic floor with representations of lions and birds, and parts of its altar. There are also remains of basilicas at Cap de Fort (near Fornells) and on the islet of Colom, near Es Grau.

Roman remains

In addition to the above, there are a variety of other Roman remains; for example, a villa mosaic floor (now housed in the Mahón museum) from the Isla del Rey. Ten Roman inscriptions have been found at Mahón, and twenty—in poor condition—in caves at Cales Coves.

A magnificent bronze statue of the Emperor Tiberius was found in the eighteenth century during the French occupation from 1756 to 1763. After changing hands several times, it was presented to Louis XV of France, and is now in the Bibliothèque Nationale, Paris. A statue of the god Mars with sword and helmet was found at the medieval fortified farmhouse of Santa Teresa near the Roman port of Sanitja previously mentioned.

The Roman occupation ended in AD 427 with the collapse of their Empire.

VANDALS AND BYZANTINES

During the following 800 years, many masters subjected Minorcans to long periods of travail, with only brief intervals of respite. The island's sovereignty was often incidental to a wider conquest elsewhere, and Minorcans had no say in their fate. Shortly after the departure of the Roman garrisons, the Vandals occupied the Balearics and persecuted the Christians in Minorca, desecrating their basilicas. This continued for over a hundred years, when the Byzantines defeated the Vandals in North Africa and Minorca then became automatically part of the Byzantine Empire.

This new regime was more peaceful, and the island's churches were restored. The baptismal font at Son Bou is believed to belong to this period, as is also the altar at Torelló. Life continued in this way for three generations, when the pendulum swung again. At the end of the seventh century the Byzantine Empire, and consequently Minorca, fell to a greater power—the Moors and Islam.

THE MOORISH PERIOD

The period of Moorish sovereignty lasted almost as long as the Roman one, but differed in character and effects. Minorcans were subject to the whims of whichever ruler held sway at the time, and these were often cruel. The Balearics were at first only nominally taken over as a result of Arab expansion in North Africa, and no attempt to occupy or even govern Minorca was made for over two hundred years. The islanders went into hiding when they saw the dreaded triangular lateen sails of the Moors, who only considered the island a useful one to raid, and from which to carry off slaves. During this period a raid came from another unexpected source; the Normans in their longships.

Minorca was first occupied by the Moors in the tenth century by Islam-el-Jaulani for the Caliphs of Cordoba. Their overlordship was not soo severe, and in 1015, when the Muslim King of Denia occupied the island, Christians were allowed complete religious freedom. But this religious tolerance did not last long, and by 1203 the whole population was Muslim. The Moors called Minorca by yet one more name, Minurka, and the town of Ciudadela was known as Medina-Minurka. They also fortified the hill of Santa Agueda.

The Moors have left few buildings in spite of their long occupation, all their mosques having been demolished by the Christians who succeeded them, building churches on the same sites. In the cathedral at Ciudadela, for instance, the base of the bell-tower is the lower part of a former minaret. In Mahón there is a single narrow arched street—Es Pont d'es General—believed to be Moorish, such as one more often sees in the *souks* of Tangier.

The real legacies of the Moors are subtle and insubstantial, and yet more lasting. A love of horses that lives on in the colourful processions during the island's fiestas, the names of beaches such as Binibeca and Santa Galdana, a love of poetry and legends like that of the Xoroi caves near Cala'n Porter. To this cave (now a discothèque and tourist attraction), situated high in the cliff face between sky and sea, a shipwrecked pirate in olden times took a Minorcan maiden whom he had stolen. Sadness at her loss reigned in her village. Ten years later a rare fall of snow revealed on the clifftop footsteps leading down to the cave, and the villagers attempted a rescue. They retrieved their daughter, and Xoroi the one-eared pirate and his eldest son threw themselves to their death into the sea.

THE HOUSE OF ARAGON

Early in the thirteenth century a new and important master for Minorca was waiting in the lists. In 1212 the small Christian kingdoms in northern Spain had at last united under the House of Aragon, and successfully challenged the Moorish usurpers, just north of Granada. Elated by this success, King Pedro II of Aragon vowed to rid the Balearics of the infidel, but it fell to his son King Jaime I to fulfil the promise.

Majorca had fallen to Jaime's armada in 1230, and when he was in that island two years later to quell a rebellion, his commander suggested that a show of force would probably bring about the surrender of Moorish Minorca without a fight. Numerous fires were lit on Majorca at a point clearly visible from Minorca, so as to suggest a large army, and the ruse was successful. As he could not spare troops for a permanent occupation, he was content with an annual tribute, which also spared Minorcans another foreign occupation. The arrangement appears to have worked well for about fifty years. King Jaime wrote in his chronicle: 'every year we received pleasant gifts without asking'.

In 1287, following treachery by Minorcans, his grandson Alphonso III decided to occupy the island.

The operation began badly. His fleet set out from Salou in Majorca, where he had spent Christmas, but his ships were scattered by a violent storm as he approached Cap Artuig at the south-western tip of Minorca. He took shelter but wearied of waiting for them to reassemble, and reached Port Mahón on 5 January with only twenty ships. There he waited another twelve days, then opened battle without them. The traditional site of the battle is flat land just to the north of Mahón known as 'dels Verges'. It was San Antonio's Day—17 January—and after the battle Pedro built a shrine with this name on the hillside just opposite the town, on which the Villa of San Antonio or the 'Golden Farm' was later built. After fierce fighting he was victorious, and the Moors retired to their fort on San Agueda. The whole island surrendered four days later.

The terms meted out to the vanquished were severe. With the exception of the Moorish governor and his entourage and family, all inhabitants who could not buy their freedom were deported as slaves, their number including many Moorish children who were forcibly separated from their parents. Shiploads of these deported slaves never saw land again, but were just tipped overboard on the high seas.

Sixty years later—on 22 July 1345—Minorca was officially incorporated in the Crown of Aragon, when Pedro IV of Aragon was at the same ceremony crowned King of Majorca and the other Balearics. This is an important date for Minorca, for by this act it became for the first time, after a history of thousands of years in which it had been nourished from roots in the Eastern Mediterranean and Africa, part of Spain as we recognise it today.

In spite of this hopeful start, Minorca had other troubles during the remainder of the Middle Ages. Plague, smallpox and cholera were often widespread, as the people were particularly prone to infection from passing ships. In 1427, when the population had been decimated, their ruler in Spain pardoned convicts for the privilege of emigrating to Minorca, and soon every cave housed a bandit.

Pirates

But the greatest scourge of the sea was piracy, which had been endemic in the Mediterranean from the earliest times. Minorcans themselves had been founder members of the art, but later they were more often on the receiving end of attacks. The climax came with the virtual destruction of Mahón by the archpirate Barbarossa in 1535, and a like destruction of Ciudadela by the Turks in 1558.

In September 1535 a fleet flying the colours of the Emperor Charles V entered the port, and the townsmen prepared to welcome the ally. When it was found to be Barbarossa flying false colours, the gates of the then-walled town were closed, and the small population prepared to defend themselves against double their numbers of invaders. Mahón fell a few days later after great slaughter, and 600 captives were sold into slavery.

In 1558 a Turkish fleet of 140 ships under Mustapha Piali attacked Ciudadela and landed 15,000 troops. Minorcans could not raise more than 700 armed men, but put up a gallant defence within the walled town. The invaders razed much of the town to the ground, butchering the inhabitants or selling them into slavery. The obelisk in the Borne Square commemorates their gallant defence.

After these two major onslaughts, the building of the new Fort St Philip at Mahón commenced, with smaller forts at Ciudadela and Fornells. Because of pirates, many Minorcans evacuated their coastal villages as being too dangerous, and settled on inland sites which have become the smaller towns of today.

In the beginning of the seventeenth century, piracy became more complex and highly organised, and was often carried out in the name of religion. On the one hand were the Muslim Barbary Corsairs and Turks, on the other the Christian Corsairs and Knights of Malta. A more respectable form of lawlessness at sea were the armed merchantmen or privateers of the various powers, licensed by their rulers to plunder enemy ships or seize their passengers, whose lives were relatively safe, but who were released at a fixed tariff. Gentlemen hurriedly unloaded their jewellery on to female passengers, who were completely safe from molestation. The alternative to ransom was to be sold as a galley slave. Only renegades could be hanged at the yard-arm at the Captain's discretion.

BRITAIN ENTERS THE MEDITERRANEAN

It was into this hornet's-nest that Britain was drawn early in the seventeenth century, to protect her growing trade with the Levant and India, and this soon led to a close association with Minorca. British merchants themselves had petitioned James I in 1617 for protection, and the first British naval squadron entered the Mediterranean shortly after. We read that in 1620 and 1621 Admiral Sir Robert Mansell 'put about for Minorca and took in wood and water'.

Britain's arrival in the 'Great Sea' was an historic event. She had absorbed in the past much of the Mediterranean culture of Greece and Rome and was now unwittingly returning to the source of that inspiration.

The sudden violence of Mediterranean storms soon turned Britain's attention to the possibility of Port Mahón as a base. Oliver Cromwell had been among the first to suggest it, but it was Charles II who negotiated treaty rights for the use of Port Mahón as early as 1664. We read that he instructed Sir Richard Fanshaw, Ambassador in Madrid, 'to request immediate permission for British ships to use Balearic ports and particularly Port Mahón'. The immediate result was that the British Navy found at their disposal, for the first time, an ideal winter base and repair and victualling depot within the Mediterranean.

From then on the Union flag was seen increasingly in Port Mahón, and British sailors were a common sight in the walled town. Mahón became a regular port of call for merchantmen sailing between England and Leghorn, and was used with great effect as a base for operations against the Algerian pirates. This arrangement continued until about 1680, during which time Minorcans and British got to know a little of each other's ways.

During this period Samuel Pepys became very familiar with Minorca through his former secretary Richard Gibson, who was then victualling officer at Port Mahón. Gibson was a prodigious worker as well as a prolific letter-writer, and we have many letters and dispatches in the Calendars of State Papers of the day, which give a vivid picture of this association, and life in Minorca at the time. Minorcans seem at last to emerge from the shadows of history, and appear as real men.

In addition, Admiral Sir Thomas Allin, a staunch Royalist who had been rewarded by Charles II with the post of commander-in-chief of the navy in the Mediterranean, described his stays in Port Mahón between punitive expeditions, in private journals which he wrote during 1669–70, and which have come down to us.

After one such expedition, we read of his return to Port Mahón on 25 October 1669:

Calm all the morning. At seven o'clock we saw the north-west end of Minorca, and the round hills which I judge to be near the centre of the island. We came to northward of the harbour, but the wind blew right out, and we could not get in. Sir Edward Spragge and those with him whom we missed from Algiers we found there [they came out to meet him]. They all came aboard, and promised to send their boats in the morning to help us in.

After an uncomfortable night at sea, they got into port next day. He continues: 'The Governor of the Castle after we had saluted his post with eleven guns and [he] answered, came in his boat to the ship's side, and desired us to go to the pratique house for health clearance, or he dared not come aboard.' When this had been done:

the Governor of the Castle first came aboard, and presently the Governor of the Island, with his son, and half a dozen grave men who stayed half an hour in compliment, offering his service in anything that lay in his powers. They took leave, having already dined, to do ten leagues to Ciudadela, as his wife lay sick. The other Governor and a Captain stayed to dinner.

On this occasion Allin made gifts to his visitors: 'to each Governor—a Moor, two quantities of fish, gloves and scarlet cloth for coats'.

There was a return invitation for Sir Thomas to the castle, of which he noted in his *Journal* afterwards: 'They treated me very civilly—and a very great dinner. Nine guns before I entered the Castle, and a guard from the port to the stairs of the Governor's lodging. And presented me in compliment the sole command as to lay down the guards' arms, and no one to enter but by my leave; and showed me the Castle.'

It was a polite charade, but no doubt pleased him. Relations were not always so friendly. Mindful of the past, the Spanish authorities on the island were nervous about too great a concentration of foreign ships in Port Mahón, lest a *coup* should follow. Richard Gibson describes his return to the island in 1670 after an absence, when he had to go ashore in a small ketch, having left the parent ship four leagues out at sea, as the Governor of the Castle would not allow more than seven or eight British ships in harbour at a time. This was contrary to the articles agreed through our ambassador in Madrid, and Sir Thomas Allin complained frequently about it to the Navy Commissioners, begging Godolphin to seek redress through court—'that Spanish friendship may be rendered something better than nothing'. The lower deck tersely stated the problem in a unique poem by John Baltharpe (an ex-galley slave) in 'The Straights Voyage', published in London in 1671:

> Good harbour this same is upon *Minork*
> For shipping very useful 'gainst the Turk.
> The King of Spain doth to our King it lend,
> As in the Line before, to that same end.
> The entrance into this same place, is not wide:
> Not 'bove a pistol shot from side to side.
>
> Likewise a Castle of great force there stands,
> Which ships as they go in and out commands.
> The Spaniards they are jealous of our Fleet.
> No more than seven a time will he admit
> For to come in, lest that we should him wrong,
> Of that same place, which he has had so long.

Another frequent grievance of British admirals was the question of gun salutes, the Spaniards demanding five British salvoes in return for only three Spanish ones. Allin and his fellow admirals usually swallowed the 'insult', as it was expedient to do so.

Sir Thomas Allin returned to England in November 1670, and was succeeded by his second-in-command Sir Edward Spragge, who successfully used Port Mahón as his base, until he too returned home in March 1672. Pepys described Allin as 'a man of known courage and service' and Spragge 'a merry man that sang a pleasant song pleasantly', which conjures up convivial occasions on board ship at Port Mahón after a successful expedition. During his time at Mahón, Spragge relied heavily on

Richard Gibson in tackling the many difficulties which arose.

Clothes for the sailors were a constant worry. Many had been clad in rags when press-ganged in England, and were now practically naked. The navy commissioners in London had introduced the issue of 'slop clothes' to combat this, but the system did not work. 'The slop-clothes are all gone', wrote Gibson to the Admiralty, 'and would there were twice as many, and more shoes and stockings for the seamen.' Sir Edward Spragge pressed the matter further in writing: 'the seamen complain for want of clothes and fall daily by agueish distempers, many being pressed men, who brought no more than is on their backs.' When more were issued, the seamen sold them for liquor, so the admiral tried issuing more wine.

In the following year he reported to Pepys that the ship *Milford*, at anchor in Port Mahón, was a total loss by fire, and the guilty seamen were given the usual punishment: 'ordered to each of them three lashes at a boat's mast, by the side of each ship riding outside the harbour's mouth'.

On another occasion he turned his house into a hospital. 'There are 100 sick and wounded ashore,' he wrote, 'to my no small trouble . . . lodging in my house.'

As Gibson turned out his endless reports for Samuel Pepys's information, he occasionally found time for a personal letter. During the stifling August heat of 1671 he explained to Pepys that Admiral Spragge allowed him 'with so great a freedom as to lay and write in his Stateroom, and to be as bold as at home'. Stretched there on a couch he promised 'a report in the island harbour of Minorca' whose 'poor but shuffling people' he found 'very friendly'. In a second, later letter, he apologises for his neglect, adding: 'I am in hopes of supplying that defect by sending your Honour a neate but large draught of the Iland.' It never arrived. For once, perhaps, Richard Gibson had a siesta.

Minorcans in 1700

While Gibson rests, a glance may be taken at the structure of Minorcan society towards the close of the seventeenth century.

At its head, as we have seen, was the Spanish governor of the island who held military and judicial responsibilities with the aid of a group of advisers. In addition there was the Governor of the Castle of Mahón, who late in the century assumed supreme powers. The pattern of society was still medieval; it was divided into gentry, military, peasants and craftsmen, the last two organised and disciplined by their respective guilds. The farms were large, and poorly husbanded. Mahón and Ciudadela were thronged with impecunious grandees and priests, and more well-to-do attorneys, notaries and doctors. The appearance of a 'poor but shuffling people' was but a reflection of the decadence and penury into which Spain had fallen at the time.

They had been touched—but only just—by their first contacts with the British, by the vigorous determination of Allin and Spragge, and by the honesty and industry of Gibson. As yet they had no inkling of the closer ties that lay ahead.

5 BRITISH DOMINION

IN the seventeenth century Britain had made uneasy use of Port Mahón to defend her trade. In the eighteenth she occupied Minorca by force for strategic reasons. These arose from her struggle with France for world empire, particularly in America. Thus, indirectly, the first tenuous threads were woven linking America with this small Mediterranean island.

The British navy had long coveted Minorca's sheltered and capacious harbour for use as a winter base. The complete naval supremacy in the Mediterranean it enjoyed during spring and summer no longer held during the winter storms. In 1694, when William III took the unpopular step of sending the main fleet to Cadiz with orders to winter there, its officers had protested at its poor shelter and lack of facilities, pressing the claims of Port Mahón anew.

With the outbreak of the War of the Spanish Succession in 1700 the way lay open to annex Minorca. Port Mahón would be invaluable as a base from which to send allied troops and war materials from Italy into Spain. In addition, the Duke of Marlborough, with that wider strategic view that befitted a great commander, knew that a strong British Minorca lying athwart the great French naval base of Toulon would prevent a junction between France's Mediterranean and Atlantic fleets (the latter based in Brest). Yet there were further delays, including an abortive attack on Toulon itself in 1707.

In the early winter of that year the murderous act of a fellow Englishman shook the Council of the Admiralty and the secretary of state, Sunderland, into action. Admiral Sir Clowdesley Shovell was returning to England as usual with his squadrons to winter and refit. He missed the English Channel altogether in a storm, and his ships were smashed against the Bishop and Clerks' Rocks in the Scilly Isles, with the loss of nine hundred officers and men. He himself, being of powerful physique and a strong swimmer, reached the shore alive. As he lay gasping exhausted in the darkness, an islander snatched off his jewelled rings, and murdered him with a knife lest he should live to tell the tale.

At last, on 13 July 1708, Marlborough wrote the long-awaited letter to Major-General Stanhope, commander-in-chief of the British forces in Spain and envoy extraordinary to Charles III of Spain. It contained Admiralty authority to secure Port Mahón for Britain forthwith, the moment and method being left to commanders on the spot. Marlborough added a postscript in his own handwriting confirming his strong views on the role of the navy in war: 'I am so entirely convinced that nothing can be done effectually without the fleet, that I conjure you to take Port Mahón.'

Minorca fell to the British ten weeks later, on 30 September 1708, as the result of a combined operation under General Stanhope and Admiral Sir John Leake (who had succeeded Shovell). Stanhope had long pressed for the event, and the navy had advocated it for sixty years. From then onwards, little Minorca was assuming a new role—a vital centre pawn on which could depend the future of North America, the West Indies and even India.

The condition of Minorcans at the time of the expedition was pitiful in the extreme. They seemed to be prone to misfortune and travail. Not only had they shared with all Spain half a century of misery and poverty under the rule of the epileptic Charles II ('The Bewitched') of Spain, but at the outbreak of the War of the Spanish Succession suffered the further agonies of a civil war.

For Spain had two kings: the seventeen-year-old Philip V of Anjou (grandson of Louis XIV of France) firmly seated in Madrid, and the fifteen-year-old Pretender Charles III (Britain's nominee from Austria), clinging precariously to Barcelona and the Catalan coast. Minorcans were predominantly in favour of Charles, but the castles at Mahón and Fornells were held by pro-Philip forces.

In October 1706 Charles's supporters gathered at the village of Mercadal in the shadow of Monte Toro, and proclaimed him their king, repeating the same declaration the following day at Ciudadela. Retribution came speedily, from Philip's General Davila, who invaded the island and ruthlessly put down the rebellion. He 'liquidated' the Minorcan intelligentsia and nobles, proscribed the national dress, desecrated the churches and denied the rights of Christian burial to the dead.

STANHOPE AND LEAKE

Both British commanders were professionals at their job: Stanhope the younger and more dashing, Leake more experienced and competent. Neither conformed to the then current type of officer who owed his position to birth and privilege.

Stanhope was born in Paris in 1673, where his father was a diplomat; he went to Oxford at the age of fourteen then joined his father in Madrid. Bent on a military career, he was sent to Italy, enlisting in the ranks. He was later commissioned as an officer in the British army and served under Marlborough in Flanders in 1703.

His portrait at Chevening, now the home of Prince Charles, shows an imposing figure with a high intellectual forehead, piercing eyes and a masterful nose and sensitive mouth. He was said to be impatient and impulsive by nature. In colouring he was swarthy; his intimate friends called him jocularly 'that handsome black man'.

Leake was born in 1656 of two generations of warrant officers in the navy, and at the outbreak of the War of the Succession had been governor and commander-in-chief of the new colony of Newfoundland. He was knighted by Queen Anne in 1703, and played a decisive part in the capture of Gibraltar in 1704.

On receipt of his instructions from the Admiralty Stanhope

had two concerns: to inform Leake as soon as possible and enlist his co-operation, and to put his own rather ragged army into a state of readiness.

As Admiral Leake was reported to be in the Adriatic, Stanhope had the Lord Treasurer's letter containing the orders copied by the hand of his secretary Cragg, and sent by a fast *felucca*, a small sailing craft, in search of him. Stanhope knew that this must be a combined operation with the navy, and in addition to telling Leake of his own preparations he requested his assistance.

> In order that no time may be lost . . . I did immediately order that 1,800 men march to Barcelona, likewise to get ready ten battering guns, some mortars, bombs, 15,000 cannon shot, and 1,000 barrels of powder. I proposed to the six men-of-war here to carry these troops as soon as they are ready for Minorca in time for your arrival. Indeed I proceed with no other hope than that you will come hither with the fleet . . . I hope you will spare us your marines, and crown all your successes by the reduction of this important fortress.

At this point Stanhope had an interservice hitch. He needed an escort of men-of-war for his transports, and six lay off Barcelona, but their commanders said they had no instructions from Leake. Fortunately one of the men-of-war's captains was Stanhope's brother—Captain Philip Stanhope of the *Milford*. He cut the red tape, and the others followed suit.

Such was the slowness of communications in these times that on 14 August Admiral Leake lay at anchor at Pula in the Adriatic unaware of these preparations, awaiting further orders and letters from Genoa and Leghorn. He fervently hoped these would at last contain orders to take Port Mahón and Minorca, but on the third day the ships arrived without orders, and there seemed nothing particular to do.

Then he remembered one uncompleted task: instructions from Queen Anne to demand 400,000 crowns from His Holiness the Pope, for his crime of encouraging the invasion of England by

(*left*) Taula of Trepucó:
a Bronze-Age religious
symbol unique to the
island; (*below*) talayot
at Talatí de Dalt: a
Bronze-Age tower used
in defence and possibly
as a chief's residence

Page 70 Naveta d'es Tudons, near Ciudadela: a group burial chamber shaped like an upturned boat, which is the oldest building standing in Spain: (*above*) exterior; (*below*) interior

praying for the Queen's enemies. If the demand was not instantly met, the Papal State was to be blown sky-high.

The following morning Leake held a council of his captains to decide what to do. It was at this moment that an aide dramatically interrupted proceedings with Stanhope's dispatch, and the blackmailing of the Pope was taken off the agenda.

THE BRITISH LAND IN MINORCA

Leake took immediate action and sailed from Pula the same evening (18 August), arriving off Port Mahón six days later, when he immediately blockaded the island. He arrived well before Stanhope, who did not arrive until three weeks later. Leake did not waste his time; he marked and surveyed a proposed landing place at Cala Alcaufar, 5km (3 miles) from the fort, and fetched a small quantity of stores and men from Majorca. He found out that the opposing garrison in Fort St Philip under the French General Jonquière numbered 1,000, half of them picked French marines, and the remainder Spanish. Leake's fleet standing off the island numbered thirty ships of the line, and he hoped that this show of strength together with his blockade would help to cow the inhabitants into early submission.

Leake covered Stanhope's landing of advance troops at Cala Alcaufar on 15 September, the day after the two commanders had made a *rendezvous*. In a mutilated letter in the British Museum from a junior officer, Cornet John Cope, to his absentee Colonel Raby, we have an 'on the spot' account of the landing and the operation. (This was the future General John Cope, the commander-in-chief routed at Prestonpans in Scotland in the Jacobite Rebellion of 1745.)

Minorca,
from the Castle of St
Philip before Port Mahón
Sept. 29, 1708

... About 2 the General landed, a great distance from the Castle, and marched himself at the head of 100 Grenadiers near three miles up the island without opposition; where we lay that night, the soldiers on their arms. The following day we disembarked most of our Forces, which then did not count above 2,000 men. The head people of the Town of Mahón came to pay obedience to the General which he excepted [sic], and in the afternoon went to take possession of it, which he secured by leaving 100 men. The 16th we marched something nearer the Castle fort and got some marines from the Fleet, that we made a body of 2,500 men, and began to disembark our Cannon.

At this stage Leake was in a dilemma, although in no doubt how to resolve it. Winter with its dangerous storms was not far off, and he was under orders from the Admiralty to proceed home with the fleet as soon as possible lest the tragedy of Shovell be repeated. Having covered the landing, and given Stanhope both marines and stores, he decided to leave a strong squadron of ships under his second-in-command, Sir Edward Whittaker, and himself proceed home. This consisted of 26 ships (18 ships of the line and frigates, 1 fire ship, 2 bomb vessels, 2 hospital ships, and 3 Dutch ships). Some of these quickly secured the surrender of the castles of Fornells and Ciudadela.

Stanhope was critical of Leake's early departure, but on the evidence Leake did efficiently all that was necessary, left Stanhope adequate help and acted correctly. In addition to Whittaker, Stanhope had the assistance of two extremely competent senior officers, Brigadier Wade, the famous road-builder in the Scottish Highlands in the '45 Rebellion, and Colonel Pettit, an engineer.

The disembarkation of the siege-train of forty-two heavy guns and fifteen mortars and their transport over rocky terrain took twelve days. 'The country is nothing but rocks and stone walls,' complained Cope. A nearer landing-stage was chosen, but this

72

was under enemy fire. The marines constructed a rough road. Others pressed on with setting up gun batteries before the fort. 'The Generall himself stayed in the Battery every night till 12 o'clock to forward the Work.'

When the attack came, the battle was fierce and of short duration. At dawn on the 28th, the general opened fire from a battery of nine guns against the two middle towers of a line-wall which had been hastily built by the defenders outside the main defences of the fort. He demolished the two towers, and breached the line-wall, which he determined to attack the following day. But the excitement of battle hastened events. Some of Brigadier Wade's Grenadiers on the right flank advanced to the breach in the line-wall without orders, and penetrated it. The brigadier had no alternative but to follow in strength in their support. The general, hearing the fire, also advanced, and the enemy retired, abandoning the other two towers. Stanhope and Wade consolidated these gains, and remained all night at the foot of the *glacis* of St Philip's Fort.

In the heat of this attack Stanhope suffered severe personal tragedy. His brother, Captain Philip Stanhope, was struck by a cannon-ball in the head while peering over the line-wall, and died. But the general continued to lead his men personally on horseback, 'exposed to the enemies' cannon, smallshot and bombs'.

Of this personal loss he was later to write in his official dispatch to the Admiralty these words:

> The conquest has cost me very dear, but since Philip died in doing service to Her Majesty and his country, I shall think his life well bestowed, as I should my own.

On the following morning (29 September) the enemy sent a small boy into the British camp as a spy, and Stanhope found time to order a leaflet campaign:

> The Generall ordered a great quantity of papers to be writ that all those who would desert should have two pistols each. Half he

writ in Spanish and the rest in French, and sewd them all round the boy, tied his hands behind him, and sent him back to the Castle.

The end came quickly the same day. The allied heavy artillery breached the main walls, and the invaders poured into the exterior defences of the fort. In the evening

> ... the enemy left off firing, sending a drum to ensure a cessation of arms, and have some of our officers come to the Castle, upon which the General ordered Major Killingrew and Captain Moysier to go with the drum.

Jonquière decided to surrender.

When Brigadier Wade accepted surrender from Jonquière inside the castle, he was astonished to find a large British cannonball on Jonquière's table. The whole operation had lasted three weeks, and there were only forty British casualties. The French were furious, for they wanted Minorca for themselves, and had Jonquière imprisoned.

In his dispatch to the Admiralty after the conquest Stanhope expressed the opinion: 'England ought never to part with this island, which will give the law to the Mediterranean in time of war and peace.'

PERFIDIOUS ALBION

Stanhope had occupied Minorca in the name of Charles III, but was determined that Britain should have it for herself. He took immediate steps to bring this about, evacuating all Spanish troops and admitting only British ones to the fort. A puppet Spanish governor was set up at the other end of the island at Ciudadela to soothe Charles, and he appointed Colonel Pettit, his senior engineer, as interim governor of the castle, who was thus able from the start to use his skill in strengthening Fort St Philip. He kept writing to Sunderland and Marlborough almost defiantly: 'Let who will be King of Spain, we should temporise in the matter, but have it yielded absolutely to us,' adding, 'I cannot give a greater demonstration of the opinion I have of this considerable acquisition for England, than by offering to stay and live here three or four years, to put it in order.'

Sunderland and his government agreed willingly to the plot, suggesting he bring pressure on Charles to cede Minorca formally to Britain, as 'some sort of security' for all her expenses on his behalf. Stanhope started a war of nerves against Charles. He told the king his whole cause and throne would collapse without British support, and to deny him at his peril. In April 1709 Charles's ministers handed over Minorca as a 'mortgage security' for the expenses Britain had incurred in fortifying Fort St Philip, from which Charles of course derived no benefit. Stanhope had written to England asking that a very high figure should be quoted, 'to put the island out of possibility of being redeemed'.

When the War of the Spanish Succession ended in 1713, Minorca and Gibraltar passed legally to the British Crown, under the Treaty of Utrecht, and the Second Duke of Argyll was appointed the first governor of the new British dominion. Gibraltar remains British today by that same treaty, but Minorca was to change hands many times until it finally became Spanish in 1802.

The Treaty of Utrecht has been generally agreed by historians to have been a disgraceful act, deserting the hapless Charles, and leaving him to fend for himself. It is said that the British troops in Barcelona just could not believe it and wept.

KANE AS GOVERNOR

The small new jewel in the British crown shone for the most part brightly. The Minorcan historian Hernández Sanz wrote in 1903: 'In July 1713, our beautiful island became a colony of Great Britain.' Minorcans drew little comfort from the clause that if Britain should ever relinquish it voluntarily it would pass again to Spain. He relates how the Duke of Argyll 'with skill and sweet words' tried to coax them to settle in the new capital at

Mahón; but Sanz felt that the suffering they had undergone for nearly two generations had induced intertia and revived a fatalism that left them ill-prepared for the vigorous rule of Britain.

This rule was paternal but strict, differing from British policy in other island dominions like the West Indies, which was often prompted by greed for gold and traffic in slaves. Minorca was not a direct source of wealth, but the possession of its harbour made the acquisition of wealth possible elsewhere. The home administration decided that the best way to retain Port Mahón was to improve the social conditions of Minorcans, and thus gain their co-operation. Much required to be done, but as so often happens the occasion produced the leader.

Colonel Richard Kane became lieutenant-governor of Minorca in 1712, and held that appointment or that of governor for twenty-five years, with the exception of two years when he held the same post in Gibraltar. He died in office in Mahón in 1736 at the age of seventy-six, and was an example for all that later came to be considered best in colonial governors. He was a professional soldier of proved merit, who had commanded at Malplaquet; he had written works on military history, drill and tactics. Now he turned swords into ploughshares. He devoted himself selflessly to the welfare of the islanders, for whom he had a genuine affection. In their religious processions he took his place with their own leaders and not as head of the occupying power. His writings are impersonal, and reveal nothing of the man. No engraved portrait of him exists, and the likeness in this book is from his statue by Rysbrack in Westminster Abbey.

In the early days of the British dominion, Minorcans had been granted freedom to practise the Catholic religion, and to retain their own laws and privileges; the island was divided into four *terminos* (districts) having a council of *jurats* (magistrates), presided over by a nobleman, and there was a Council for the whole island, the *Universidad*, which dealt with taxation and petitions to the ruling power. After the Treaty of Utrecht in 1713, certain difficulties required resolution and Britain sent a commissioner,

Henry Neal, to the island to hear the complaints and proposals of Minorcans, and this was followed by a delegation of two leading Minorcans to England. Kane, who happened to be on furlough, was called in consultation. In due course, in 1714 (shortly after the death of Queen Anne), the delegates returned to Minorca, laden with royal ordinances and a large measure of local self-government.

On Kane's return he was distressed to find that tactless behaviour of some of his officers had caused a worsening of relations between Britains and Minorcans, and that violence against British troops had occurred, setting off the new measures to a bad start. Most serious was the murder by Minorcans of three British soldiers near Albufera Lake. The culprits were never found, and Kane levied a punitive fine of 500 gold dubloons on the local authorities, which he later remitted, though he never forgave the crime. Later, when a peasant in the same area was murdered by a soldier, he opened a subscription list for the widow, and himself contributed £90.

Like the Roman proconsuls Kane was a road builder, and between 1713 and 1720 built what is still known as Cami d'en Kane (Kane's Road) from Fort St Philip to Cuidadela. It was soundly constructed, mostly over 30ft wide, and entailed the draining of the marshes at the head of Port Mahón, which subsequently became (as they are today) a large and fertile orchard, vegetable and market garden. It was here that Minorcans themselves first raised a monument in honour of Kane in 1926, which was replaced by a new one in 1972. It was essentially a military road, for although the capital was to be moved to Mahón, a small garrison was retained in Ciudadela, and detachments were moved by road. It ran to the north of the town of Alayor, instead of the south as the present one does.

His second most important act was consolidation of the removal of the capital from Ciudadela, in view of the importance of Port Mahón. He himself had taken up residence in the Vila a Castell de Mahón (Town and Castle of Mahón), but it was not until 1721 that he issued an order that the Minorcan law courts

77

and their officers should take up residence with their families. This step led to a partial decline of Ciudadela, and had a profound effect on the expansion and increased importance of Mahón. With the increased prosperity of the new dominion, Mahón soon burst its walls, which Kane partially demolished. He carried out extensive town-planning, building new streets like George Street (now known as Calle de San Jorge) and widening old ones, like Hannover Street, named after George I. He also increased the facilities of the port, building workshops and warehouses.

As a crowning achievement he rebuilt St Philip's Fort, honeycombing it with underground passages like a Maginot Line. Since it ultimately cost the British exchequer over £1,000,000, and was constructed on the principles of the master Vauban, it was rightly believed to be one of the finest fortresses in Europe. He also built the smaller Marlborough Fort at Cala Esteban (also known as St Stephen's Cove).

Fighting inflation

Throughout this period Kane also devoted much time to improving the economic and social life of Minorcans, tackling the problem of inflation, which arose from the immense amount of money pouring into the island to maintain and feed the garrison.

He based his measures on an accurate study of the population and their assets, conducting a detailed census in 1723. In addition to the numbers of men and women, he counted men of military age, estates, wells, rents, even livestock. The population then numbered 16,082. Turning farmer, he imported cattle and sheep for breeding, as well as food, together with poultry and eggs from France, Italy and Barbary, which he distributed to farmers. He also introduced the deep red vetch ('sulla') from Italy as fodder, that one still sees growing waist-high on Minorcan hillsides. Sometimes he had disasters, as in 1732 when the island lost 16,000 livestock through lack of fodder caused by drought. But in spite of this and the extra mouths to feed,

Minorcans enjoyed a prosperity they had never known. Production of wine, vegetables and fowls increased by 500 per cent in
the first forty years of the new dominion's life, and by 1752
Minorca had 7,000 cattle, 60,000 sheep, 2,000 goats and 4,000
swine. Kane's stewardship extended to instructions as to the
correct manner of reaping crops, and he checked on his measures
for control of the prices of food by daily visits to the Mahón
market. Standardised weights and measures from England
prevented short measure.

Like Richard Gibson in a humbler post fifty years earlier,
Kane's stamina and industry in an often enervating climate fills
one with admiration, but his work was not made easier by two
flaws which began to show in the British jewel. These were the
growing indiscipline of British troops and a clerical revolt which
encouraged terrorist acts by Minorcans against them.

The clerical revolt

This revolt was inevitable, for Minorca like Spain was Catholic, while Britain after centuries of religious strife was aggressively
Protestant. Before the British occupation in 1708 Minorcan
priests came under the jurisdiction of their superiors in Majorca,
and the latter resented Kane's usurping their authority. Kane
made his wishes known by executive orders, in which the
sanctuary of felons in churches and the practice of the Inquisition
were forbidden. But perhaps the Catholic clergy found it most
difficult to obey the command: 'all the clergy shall pray for His
Britannic Majesty'.

Many of the clergy, encouraged by the Bishop of Majorca,
encouraged disaffection. Soldiers found alone were attacked
with knives, or even stoned to death. Kane dealt sternly with
these outbreaks, giving orders that persons with prohibited arms
or guilty of stoning 'be flogged in the middle of the square by the
hangman's hand'. The carrying of pointed knives was forbidden,
and possession of arms could lead to three months' imprison-
ment. Parents were asked to discourage their children from
stone-throwing. There was a grim reminder of sterner penalties

79

in another order: 'if gallows are knocked down or broken, or if the body of the malefactor be taken down from it', the citizens had to deliver up the culprit or suffer a collective fine.

During this period Kane continued his social policy. Minorcan children were given free education at English schools should this be desired by their parents, and the clergy were warned that if they discouraged or prevented it they would be expelled from the island. It is clear from documents at this time that Britain had no intention of relinquishing Minorca as a dominion, but planned to colonise it with British families and even hoped it would ultimately become Protestant. Kane received from his absentee superior in England, Lord Carpenter, a document entitled 'Proposals for securing a Protestant Interest on His Majesty's Island of Minorca', according to which troops and officers could settle on the land, but would continue to receive their army pay. Loans and grants would be given for stock, and they would only be recalled to military duty in an emergency. Minorcans got to hear of the scheme, and feared they would be dispossessed. Nothing came of it.

In 1720 a certain Don Jean de Bayerre petitioned the British government on behalf of the islanders against Kane's rule, and the alleged excesses of British troops. Kane was exonerated. Details are given in a pamphlet published in 1720 entitled *A Vindication of Colonel Kane, Lieut Governor of Minorca, against complaints by the Inhabitants of the Island.*

A glance at one of the twenty-eight complaints and answers in the pamphlet adds to the picture of life in Minorca at this time.

One Saint's day, the congregation worshipping in the church of Santa Maria in Mahón had some unusual excitement. A thief escaping from his pursuers sought illegal sanctuary in the dimly lit church. A British officer of the Guard, seeing him enter, followed him inside, accompanied by a sergeant, in order to seize him. Uproar followed, the priests leaving the altar, attempting to protect him. Although the officer and sergeant did not retaliate with force, 'at the same time a Spanish gentleman, a stranger that had served in the army in Spain, being in the church, attempted to draw his sword against the British officer: but he being seized was sent in arrest to St Philip's Castle'. The clergy complained that a member of the congregation had been molested, to which Kane gave the cutting reply 'that the officer had done his duty, and that if he had not been a very young officer, he would have run his sword through the Gentleman'.

Nothing is known of Kane's personal life. It appears unlikely that he married. He died in Minorca at the age of seventy-six, on 19 December 1736, and was buried at his request in Fort St Philip. Owing to later demolitions, the location of his grave is not now known. His only biography is a slim Spanish volume published in 1924 by Antonio Victory. It covers only the Minorcan part of his career. Minorcans still remember Kane as a good governor, who had their interests at heart.

JOHN ARMSTRONG'S MEMOIRS OF MINORCA

The first British occupation of Minorca produced two chroniclers who have left valuable accounts of garrison and civilian life on the island during that period. These were 'Engineer in Ordinary' John Armstrong and Dr George Cleghorn, whose account of the climate of Minorca we have already read.

Armstrong arrived in Minorca early in 1738 on a tour of duty lasting four years. During this time he collected material and drafted his book (written in the form of letters) *A History of the Island of Minorca*, which has become a classic on life in the eighteenth century in 'a remote part of His Majesty's Dominions'. It was completed at his Chelsea home in 1752.

Little is known about Armstrong apart from the internal evidence of his book. From his carefree life on the island he was probably a bachelor at the time, perhaps in his middle twenties. The Royal Engineers were not founded till 1787, and he was one of a small cadre of civilian engineers who were attached to artillery units, mainly to look after ordnance.

In addition to history, natural history and topography, he gives a detailed account of Minorcans as he saw them, and went about his task with praiseworthy industry. 'I had not been long there,' he writes, 'before I had acquired a competent Skill in their Language, to enable me to converse with the Natives . . . I contrived to make all my excursions and parties of pleasure, with my Friends, subservient to my Designs.'

Garrison life

In peacetime five British regiments were stationed in Minorca. Mahón was the military headquarters, and there were detachments at Alayor, Fornells and Ciudadela. At Mahón each officer had a house assigned to him, while other ranks were accommodated in houses requisitioned from unwilling families who were paid compensation in return. The idea of barracks was still a new one, and this form of permanent billeting was then common. The town authorities were also required to provide each man with a ration of wood and oil, of which Armstrong writes: 'A Subaltern's Allowance of Oil is sufficient for one Lamp, and his Wood with very good management will boil his Tea-kettle two mornings in the Week.' A lot of complicated sharing must have taken place.

Of his average day at Mahón, he says:

I have a good House, decently furnished. I rise early and breakfast alone, then write and draw till Noon. It is then time to dress, after which I walk till Dinner is ready at a Publick-house at one; where eight of us who like one another, eat very well for twelve Shillings a Week, finding our own Wine, which costs only three halfpence a Bottle, and is very good. After Dinner we walk again, or make a Party at Cards, or to the Gardens, and so to Supper at eight o'clock.

On more formal occasions:

At our Mess we seldom dine without a Soup and dish of Fish, with a couple of other things, as a piece of Beef, a joint of Mutton, a Turkey, Goose, Ducks, Fowls, wild and tame Rabbits, a Pudding or a Pye, with plenty of Roots, Greens and Fruits, all according to the Season. We have very good French Bread, Cheese from England, and Butter from Ireland . . .

In the cooler months of the year officers went on numerous pleasure excursions by mule, and were sometimes accompanied by their families: 'there is scarce an Officer among us whose house does not afford a spare bed for his Friends, even for a month or six weeks, where you are treated with great Cheerfulness'. The whole picture is one of comparative ease and expectation of permanence. But in his last chapter Armstrong mentions an occasional misgiving that old service officers will recognise: 'Here my Youth passes in Obscurity and Indolence, my Friends grow old and my pretensions forgot, while my juniors are promoted by being on the Scene, and my letters make little impression in my Absence.'

This comfortable picture takes no account of the very different lives of the 'other ranks'. There had been little improvement since the days of Allin and Spragge, and in the mid-eighteenth century troopships such as existed for transport of troops to Minorca have been described by a contemporary writer as: 'floating slaughter-houses'. The wastage of men at sea was appalling: up to half a ship's complement could be lost by sickness on a long voyage, a situation as advantageous to the enemy as a sea victory.

Recruits were often professional criminals, fraudulently enlisted, or press-ganged. Once on the island the prospect of home leave was extremely remote. Owing to a surviving Tudor tradition, a regiment became irretrievably attached to a particular base, and a regiment might remain unrelieved for up to sixty years. Such garrisons overseas were often shockingly neglected— as was Minorca in the 1750s—and even forgotten. Entries in a warrant book at this period read: 'the fortifications are as in ill condition as the quarters, and the unhappy soldiers beg in vain for new bedding to replace that which had worn out by ten years of service'.

In spite of the difficulty of escaping by sea, soldiers sometimes deserted. Having broken barracks, they made for the country and lived off the land. Ferrerias was a favourite goal as there was no garrison there, though later a barracks was built (it is now the country house of Son Telm) to house a permanent guard of dragoons. From there deserters would make their way through the rugged defile of Algendar to the beaches of Galdana or Macarella which were nearest Majorca, where they stole a boat or forced a Minorcan at knife-point to sail them across.

For their own protection Minorcans were given powers by the governor to arrest any soldier trespassing on their land, and were advised to secure their boats against theft. For failure to report the presence of a soldier, they themselves would be punished. Thefts of produce from the land became a capital offence, and when two soldiers were sentenced to death in Fort St Philip in 1755 for doing so the Court with unusual generosity allowed them to cast lots for their lives, and only hanged one.

The Duke of Argyll, writing in *Parliamentary History* in 1742 on conditions in Minorca, expressed the opinion that 'A long term of duty at Mahón was equivalent to a punishment, and my only surprise was that the troops had not mutinied.' The Duke did not often go himself.

Nothing is known of the latter part of Armstrong's life or when he died. He is worthy of remembrance for his excellent 'Correct Map of the Island of Minorca' as well as his book. He has left no portrait but a signed silhouette of his head in profile, which shows an ageing, portly man.

A DOCTOR IN MINORCA

But one terror struck all ranks, and Minorcans too: illness and epidemics that brought death. The following letter from a naval officer to Jolliffe Tufnell, of Langley near Chelmsford (preserved in the Bodleian Library at Oxford) vividly describes the prevailing conditions:

Sept. the 16th Old Style
1740, at Sea

Dearest Brother,

I shall now give you an account of what passes with us, as we have no other news in these parts.

One of the most material is how narrowly we escaped the Plague at Mahón by a French *settee* from Algiers, where the Plague rages very fiercely. Coming into the harbour, Major de Maw, belonging to St Philip's, going abroad to buy some things, when he was alongside saw one man upon deck with his head muffled up. On enquiring, he had one of the plague glands on his throat. And the rest of the men being all sick of it, they were ordered to leave the Harbour immediately which they did.

In case the officer had not been in the produce boat himself, for a little money they would have admitted them.

A spotted fever [smallpox] has raged all over the fleet in a manner almost as bad, taking off twelve or thirteen men daily; so that Mr. Haddock's fleet has buried twelve hundred and upward.

Dear Brother, most affectionately yrs.

George Tufnell

It was not without reason that British troops christened the King's Island in Port Mahón on which the military hospital was built 'Bloody Island'.

Dr George Cleghorn, MD, arrived in Minorca to tackle such problems in 1736, as surgeon to the 22nd Regiment of Foot. He was a brilliant physician, and during a tour of duty that lasted thirteen years distinguished himself as a clinician and research worker on Mediterranean diseases. He was born near Edinburgh in 1716, and at an early age showed a remarkable gift for the classics; his later medical treatises were written in Latin. At the age of fifteen he resolved to study physic and surgery, a fortunate choice as the Edinburgh Medical School was at that time, together with Leyden, unrivalled in Europe.

As was then the custom he was apprenticed to a doctor, the famous Alexander Monro, as his personal pupil. He lived in Monro's home, where he was joined a few years later by Dr James Fothergill, who guided him in the earlier part of his career. At the age of twenty, he was posted as surgeon to Minorca, under the command of General St Clair.

Whatever time could be spared from his official duties Cleghorn employed by investigating the nature of epidemic diseases as modified by climate, and in gratifying his passion for anatomy and dissection. In the meantime his good friend Dr Fothergill was indefatigable in searching the London shops for the books he wanted, and sending them to him as best he could.

The commonest diseases then prevalent were plague, cholera and smallpox, typhoid, pneumonia, malaria and gastro-intestinal diseases. The even tenor of life and relaxed existence of British officers' families on the 'Summer Island' was often broken by serious illness and death.

Smallpox was brought from Constantinople by one of His Majesty's ships in 1745, and spread over the whole island. Cleghorn wrote: 'It carried off nearly all the children who survived the chin-cough [whooping cough?] and the summer fever.' There had been a previous epidemic in March 1742, with many deaths among both English children and soldiers, so that 'every house might be called a hospital'. The hot summer months were generally considered unhealthy for children, many dying from cholera and tertian fever (malaria).

Although the connection between malaria and the mosquito was then unknown, Cleghorn was already using cinchona bark (quinine) in the treatment of this fever, and mosquito nets were in regular use. 'Of all our Insects,' wrote Armstrong, 'this Musquita is the most troublesome, and if it were not for the Canopies of Gauze and Muslin with which our beds are constantly enclosed during the hot Months, it would be impossible to get a night's rest.'

Cleghorn sent the records of his research regularly to his friend Fothergill, but it was not until his return to England in 1749 that his colleague helped him put his notes together in English for publication in 1750 of his book *Observations on the Epidemical Diseases in Minorca from 1744 to 1749*. This went through four editions. In the latter part of his life he was Lecturer in Anatomy at the University of Dublin. His portrait shows him as a kindly, studious man.

Page 87 (above) Prehistoric street in Torre d'en Gaumés, which shows remains of dwellings; (below) remains of Byzantine Basilica on shore at Son Bou, which dates from fifth century AD. Note the circular megalithic font in the background

Page 88 (*above*) Roman mosaic from Basilica at Torelló, discovered by a farmer in 1956 when clearing the field of stones; (*below*) Phoenician (and later Roman) port at Sanitja in the north, dating from about 1500 BC

THE VISIT OF SIR JOSHUA REYNOLDS

Returning to happier themes, no better illustration of the apparent stability and permanence of Minorca as a British dominion can be given than by relating an intriguing event on the island in 1749, shortly after Cleghorn's departure.

On 18 August of that year a naval vessel signalled and anchored off Quarantine Island, with an unusual visitor on board.

The British garrison, accustomed to the comings and goings of military and naval officers of high rank, took little notice of the arrival of a young man of twenty-six—a civilian—of no apparent rank or substance. Yet he was destined for fame and wealth, being none other than the future Sir Joshua Reynolds.

Reynolds's little-known visit to Minorca occurred on his way to Italy, where he planned to study the portrait painting of Raphael and Michelangelo. Reynolds was gifted but poor, and the realisation of his plan had seemed an impossible dream. His visit came about by a strange intervention of nature, and lasted for five months, owing to a second fortuitous happening. Minorca left its mark on Reynolds for life.

On 25 April, Reynolds had been staying with his friend Lord Edgcumbe, at the latter's home near Plymouth, painting portraits of his family. Edgcumbe, himself a young man, and destined to play an important naval part in Minorca seventeen years later, had taken a liking to Reynolds, and Reynolds had told him of his dream.

Even as he spoke, a more famous young naval officer, Commander Keppel, bound for the Mediterranean in the *Centurion*, ran into a westerly gale two miles out of Spithead, and sprung both topmasts, damaging his rigging. Altering course, he put into Plymouth for repairs, and joined his friend Edgcumbe's household until these should be completed. Thus fortuitously Keppel and Reynolds met, and took an instant liking to each other.

F

As a result of this friendship Keppel offered Reynolds a berth as his personal guest on the *Centurion,* and so it was agreed. Reynolds was so poor that the problem of incidental living expenses on so long a cruise arose. His sisters Mary and Elizabeth came to the rescue, and he sailed from Plymouth on 11 May 1749.

Reynolds had never been to sea before, but quickly settled down to the leisurely routine of the voyage. The sleek, graceful *Centurion* carried a complement of 400 men, but her guns had been reduced in numbers to provide more cabin space. Keppel proved the perfect host, and Reynolds shared his spacious day cabin, with its excellent library. They put in at Gibraltar on 18 June, and before calling in at Minorca had a skirmish with the Dey of Algiers.

The *Centurion* put into Port Mahón on 18 August after a voyage of just over three months. Through Keppel's influence, Reynolds stayed at St Philip's Castle as the personal guest of the governor, the aged General Blakeney. The English ladies in the garrison were intrigued by the young painter, who was popular at their balls. Throughout the summer and autumn days he joined their pleasure excursions—mainly on mules—to the surrounding bays. But unfortunately he had a riding accident, which for some time confined him to his room, and delayed his sailing for five months.

During this period of convalescence, he is said to have painted twenty-five to thirty portraits of army and naval officers of the garrison, practically none of which have been traced. There exists one of Keppel of this period, a slim figure with hand in tunic, very different from the later portly figure. But the others are lost to posterity, and a fortune awaits their finder.

The riding accident disfigured Reynolds's face for life, and some of his self-portraits show a lip disfigurement. Only one of the letters Reynolds wrote from Minorca has survived. It was to his girl-friend in England, Miss Weston. (He never married.) In it he wrote: 'my lips are spoiled for kissing'.

THE MINORCANS IN A BRITISH DOMINION

Little has been said of the character of Britain's Minorcan subjects in the new dominion. Both Armstrong and Cleghorn agree
that Minorcans seemed indolent and unambitious. They paid
their taxes in support of the garrison uncomplainingly, with the
fatalism of a subject people, and shelved responsibility for their
welfare on the ruling power. Only a few hankered after better
things. Both writers also mention a trait that no longer exists: a
tendency to quarrel and be suspicious of each other. Nothing
could be further from the facts today. Cleghorn's detailed
account of the character of Minorcans in 1751 is worth placing
on record:

> The Natives of this Island are commonly thin, lean, and well
> built, strong and active, of a middle stature and an olive Com-
> plexion. Their hair for the most part is black and curled; in many
> Chestnut coloured; in some Red. In a word, the young People
> are either of a sanguine or cholerick Constitution; while those of
> more advanced Years, become dry, meagre, and what the
> Ancients called strabilious . . . They don't commonly live to so
> great an age as the Inhabitants of more northerly Countries . . .
> Girls soon arrive at maturity, and soon grow old . . . Both sexes are
> by constitution extremely amorous. They are often betrothed
> to each other, while children, and marry at Fourteen.

Minorcans normally lived frugally, wheat bread being more
than half their diet, and ate little meat. Fish, rice, eggs and root
vegetables were also eaten, to which they added summer fruits.
With their food they always drank wine. But at fiestas and
weddings food was lavish, and at a country farmer's wedding
which Cleghorn attended the amount eaten 'could scarcely be
credited'.

There was another side to the life of this supposedly listless
people. A full quarter of the year was devoted to holidays and
fiestas, in which the religious ceremonies took a very minor role.
Between 'harvest and vintage' there was a succession of outdoor

processions and dancing, masques, horse and foot racing, and 'all manner of sports' accompanied by castanets, pipes, violins and guitars. Oranges were thrown at lovers as in ancient Greek times, and extempore calypsos were sung by rival guitarists in competition with each other.

Dress and fashion

Minorcan everyday dress was striking and unusual. Men wore a loose short coat or jacket, a waistcoat, and red worsted girdle or wide leather belt, and beneath these a coarse shirt with coloured neckerchief, a red worsted cap, long breeches to the ankles, and broad flat shoes of white leather. Those of higher rank wore a wig, cocked hat and sword. If in mourning the latter tied a black cloth over the scabbard of his sword.

Women's everyday dress consisted of a black, close-fitting sleeved waistcoat, wide and open at the neck but closely fastened at the wrists. A coloured skirt or petticoat, full at the hips, came up over it, and was tied at the waist. This struck a gayer and quite modern note, for it only reached to mid-calf. They wore coloured woollen stockings of red, blue or green, with clocks of a different colour, white shoes with high heels, and square perforated toes; also a peasant-style headshawl, which was coyly pinned under the chin.

On formal occasions at which British and Minorcans met, a black veil fastened at the waist was brought up over the head, but not obscuring the face. The hair was gathered behind, and either plaited or tied with a coloured ribbon. It was very long and often ended in a little curl.

When greeted on a social occasion by a British officer, a woman would acknowledge it with a gentle bowing of the head. One did not touch a Minorcan lady's hand, even formally in salutation. If this seemed likely to happen, the lady's usual reply was: '*Mira y no tocas*'—'Look, and do not touch.'

6   A BELEAGUERED ISLAND

AFTER an occupation lasting forty-eight years, and in spite of a benevolent rule, Britain lost Minorca to the French in 1756, for reasons which both Stanhope and Armstrong had foreseen: Britain had failed to retain the trust and co-operation of Minorcans, largely through a difference in religion, and the strength of both naval and land forces on the island had been allowed to fall to danger level.

Writing in 1740, Armstrong pointed out that of the four regiments of foot and one of artillery totalling 2,400 men on the island the effective strength for defence of Fort St Philip was only 800, after allowing for detachments at Alayor and elsewhere, men on repair work and maintenance, sick and wounded. The fleet would therefore be a vital factor in defence, but that if 'a series of misfortunes be on our side, causing us to lose naval supremacy, I see no remedy but that this island must fall . . . in the common calamity'. The words were prophetic, for these were the conditions in which Admiral Byng failed to relieve beleaguered Minorca, which cost him his life.

The French invasion of Minorca ushered in the Seven Years War, which lasted from 1756 till 1763, but Britain was not actually at war when the French troops landed. This being so, certain eighteenth-century courtesies were first observed. General Blakeney, the British commander inside Fort St Philip, sent a drum-major to Alayor in full uniform to wait upon Marshal Richelieu, the French commander, demanding 'the reason of the French King's troops landing in a hostile manner, in His Majesty's island of Minorca'. (The drum-major was careful to note and report on the enemy's dispositions on his return.)

The Marshal dispatched his reply a few days later, sending Blakeney a gift of dried fruits. Blakeney responded with six bottles of English beer.

The Seven Years War was a world war, in which Britain and France continued their struggle for empire in North America and the East. At the time of the attack on Minorca, British fortunes were at a low ebb for she had suffered reverses in Canada, and lost Calcutta to Suraja Dowlah in the same year (1756). The loss of Minorca was a serious one for Britain. In 1756 the thirteen British colonies on the American seaboard faced a line of French forts in Canada designed to prevent the British from pushing farther west. Its loss weakened the ability of Britain to break France's long supply-lines by sea to Europe.

Britain broke the uneasy truce with France in Europe in 1755 and France replied by threatening to invade England, at the same time planning to reconquer Minorca. For the latter she amassed a large fleet and army at Toulon, and as this could not be kept secret it suited France to conduct a war of nerves against Britain.

At one moment she let it be known that this fleet was to reinforce the invasion of England, and at the next there was a 'leak' that they were destined for America. The third rumour was that Minorca was the objective, but so persistent was this that it was mostly disbelieved by the British government. During 1755 this incredulity was excusable, for it appeared the French did not know themselves. Their generals, like Hitler's in a later age, began to have doubts about an invasion of England; and Louis XV was unable to order an attack on Minorca until Madame de Pompadour had selected a commander.

The choice of Admiral Byng to take a relief force to Minorca in 1756 was made on seniority rather than merit. The Honourable John Byng was the son of a distinguished admiral—Lord Torrington—and it was not always easy to succeed the famous. At the time of his appointment he was fifty-three years of age, and had not fired a shot in anger for thirty years. He was described as plump, overbearing, and rather fussy. In his portraits he looks pompous and overdressed. But the fatal trait in his character was his dislike of responsibility, and of taking decisions.

The invasion of Minorca came on 18 April 1756, and the Duke of Newcastle and his Ministry had received warnings of naval and military troop concentrations at Toulon as early as September the previous year. But to these and other secret advices they paid no heed. It was said that the Duc de Richelieu was the French commander and the number of his force 15,000 men, but Newcastle remained convinced they were meant for elsewhere.

Not until 9 March did the Board of the Admiralty stir itself into action, and as dispatches took up to six weeks to reach Minorca by sea, General Blakeney was ignorant of any measures whatever to help him when the blow fell.

The Admiralty's action was totally inadequate and consisted of ordering a number of ships' captains to prepare their vessels for duty in the Mediterranean without delay, and not until 17 March was Vice-Admiral John Byng notified of his promotion to Admiral, and that he would command a squadron of ten ships. It also instructed the army to recall forty-one absentee officers for return to Minorca—including wives, children and servants— but no provision was made for their transport.

When Admiral Byng went on board his new flagship *Ramillies* at Portsmouth he found that his new squadron was deficient of 722 officers and men. His own flagship had a crew deficiency of 222. In spite of the urgency of his task, he found he had been allotted other duties unconnected with his preparations, and his protests to the Admiralty were ignored.

A succession of contradictory orders then reached him from the Admiralty, which was clearly in a state of panic. Following a last-minute offer of 300 men from other ships, Byng was ordered to transfer all his marines to other ships to provide space to transport 900 officers, men, servants and families of Lord Robert Bertie's Fusiliers. Lest he should think these troops might assist him in relieving Minorca, the next dispatch told him he must put them all ashore at Gibraltar. Would he also provide

95

cabins for the forty-one absentee officers from Minorca, including their families? Confusion and muddle continued till the end. Byng was to receive his final orders from Governor Fowkes at Gibraltar. He was to proceed to Minorca only if the French attacked it. Perhaps the Toulon fleet was bound for America after all, in which case he was to pursue it.

Admiral Byng put to sea from Portsmouth on 7 April 1756, only eleven days before the French attacked Minorca. He had neither fireships, hospital ship or even troop transports. There had been a few days' delay in sailing because of storms, and the *Intrepid* had belied her name by returning to port, her timbers hopelessly rotten, and leaking badly. None of his ships' complements was complete. The frustrations, contradictions and muddle in preparations for the voyage to Minorca could have shaken and disheartened any man. For one of Byng's gloomy temperament the effect would have been more traumatic and permanent.

Byng arrived at Gibraltar on 2 May after a stormy voyage that lasted thirty days; there he learned from Captain Edgcumbe of the French attack fourteen days previously. The Duc de Richelieu had landed a force of 20,000 troops from 200 transports under the Admiral Galissonnière. The British garrison under command of General Blakeney numbered only 2,800. He found the necessary naval supplies for his ships sadly lacking at Gibraltar, where the facilities for cleaning and repairing of vessels had fallen into decay. He reported these unpalatable facts to the Admiralty, who were responsible for the negligence.

A Council of War was held, at which it was decided not to embark extra personnel or war materials for Minorca, as these would probably be speedily captured. He thus lost valuable senior officers from regiments who were in the Fort of St Philip. When Byng's pitiful little fleet of leaky ships at last continued on its way to Minorca, the admiral was unaware that this was his last naval expedition. He was later tried by court-martial for losing the Battle of Mahón, and the stage was set for the Greek tragedy that was to cost him his life.

General Blakeney's chief claim to fame lies in his gallant defence of Minorca in 1756 at the age of eighty-four. Blakeney's detractors said that he conducted the seventy-day siege from his bed, as he suffered from gout.

Promotion had come late to the general, who did not become a colonel till his sixty-fifth year. St Philip's Fort was not the first he defended. During the 1745 Jacobite Rebellion—when he was seventy-two—he was Lieutenant-governor of Stirling Castle, and routed his Highland attackers. When appointed Lieutenant-governor of Minorca in 1747, he was seventy-five.

On arrival in Minorca he took over supreme command, as the governor Lord Tyrawley was absent on leave, and continued to be for the next nine years. Blakeney was far from happy about the state of his defences, and made such preparations as he could, accumulating stores in the fort against a siege, including 1,000 barrels of beef from Leghorn, which Fowkes of Gibraltar had refused. As rumours of a French attack strengthened, he called his first Council of War on 5 February 1756, to which he invited a certain naval captain, the Honourable Augustus Hervey of His Majesty's ship *Phoenix*, which happened to be in port. Hervey was critical of Blakeney, and a close friend of Byng although he disapproved of his strategy. He later staked his career in support of Byng at the latter's trial. Hervey was a colourful and flamboyant personality. In addition to being an English Casanova and a competent naval officer, he was a diarist like Pepys, with many entries describing Mahón and coming threats of war:

> *2nd May 1753*—I had but little winds and got off Mahón . . . and sailed into the harbour when the sea breeze came in. I found several of my old acquaintances: Colonel Rufane, Mr. and Mrs. Mace, Col. Lockhart and General Blakeney, whom I dined with. Mr. Edgcumbe came in and we were glad to renew old friendships. I went to the Freemason's Lodge held by brother Boyd; I was admitted member of it, and drank three times three to the Brethern of it . . . We were very merry while I stayed at Mahón, making parties at Alayor and Ciudadela, and shooting.
>
> *1st Jan. 1756*—I got into Port Mahón on New Year's Day . . . but no declaration of war yet. I found here many rich and beauti-

ful prizes [captured ships]. We sealed up all their papers and hatches, and laid them in safety. I diverted myself very well at Mahón with my friends of Cornwallis's Regiment, and was lucky enough to get in with a very pretty girl, daughter of Smallridge that kept the tavern. She and I agreed very well, and I kept her all the while, and a sweet pretty creature she was, so that she engrossed my whole time here, and as I lay at the house, we had no interruption. I prepared for sea as soon as I could, expecting war every minute. We received intelligence from all parts that the French are meditating the taking of Minorca, and assembling a great fleet and army at Toulon . . .

At a Council of War on 5 February, which sat for several weeks, Hervey was critical of Blakeney's lack of action, of the countless resolutions that were never implemented, and attributed the inertia of the aged general to his undue kindness to the inhabitants. He suggested that Minorcans who had helped in constructing the secret passages in the fort be moved inside it lest they disclose them to the enemy; that buildings too close to the fort be demolished; and that the island be placed under martial law.

The wearied general waited till he had finished, then sent him to sea to reconnoitre for the enemy. Hervey was not deceived and wrote in his diary: 'This evening I was ordered off the island for seven days to give notice of the enemy's approach' but he 'believed the General wanted to get rid of me out of the Council.'

On 16 April Blakeney received his first information of the enemy fleet's approach from a fast sloop he had sent out to reconnoitre, and on the following day from an outlook tower on Monte Toro part of the great armada had been seen off Fornells. Byng's relief expedition had sailed from England only ten days before, and was still somewhere in the Bay of Biscay. Captain the Honourable George Edgcumbe's tiny squadron at Port Mahón constituted the entire British Naval force then in the Mediterranean.

Edgcumbe placed a boom across the entrance to Port Mahón by sinking the *Proserpine* athwart it—a practice adopted at Scapa Flow in the Orkney Islands in later times. This done, he was ordered to take his little squadron off to Gibraltar to avoid inevitable capture. Edgcumbe was unhappy about this apparent desertion of his comrades, but left behind his marines, and hoped to return with Byng. Sadly the garrison watched them sail out.

Just as they sailed, another ship entered Port Mahón carrying a British officer, and a moving story emerges. He was Captain William Cunningham, formerly second engineer at Minorca, who had been wrongly passed over for promotion to chief engineer, in which capacity he had also acted. He was on his way home with his wife and children by sea. His wife was pregnant and they had put into Nice for her confinement. Here he learnt of the pending French attack, and remembered the rotten wooden gun platforms at Fort St Philip. Putting personal and family considerations aside, he decided he must return to Minorca at once, and spent all his money (£1,600) on buying timber and chartering a ship to transport it to Port Mahón, where he arrived just in time and greatly cheered the garrison.

These were not the days of total war, and he wrote soon after the attack to the enemy commander—Richelieu—about the predicament of his wife and family in an enemy country. The Duc reassured him as to their safety. Cunningham got his post as chief engineer, and was wounded in the final assault on the fort. The final capitulation terms specifically mentioned him by name, for safe conduct and repatriation for himself and family.

Blakeney at length made his final dispositions. He sunk a second sloop across the narrow entrance to the port, and outlying garrisons at Ciudadela, Fornells and Alayor were withdrawn and gathered within the fort. Belated demolition of houses abutting on the fort were carried out, and portions of Kane's road were hastily destroyed to delay the enemy's advance. Twenty-eight Minorcan bakers were recruited to bake biscuits and bread, but either from apathy or mistrust an appeal six weeks earlier for other help had produced only twenty-two volunteers—a sad reflection on almost half a century of British colonialism.

Of Blakeney's small garrison of 2,800, forty-one officers were on leave in England, including the governor, Lord Tyrawley, the Governor of Fort St Philip, all the colonels of the four regiments, and twenty-eight other officers. In addition, he had within the fort 440 British women and 291 children.

Since his officers were all comparatively junior, he decided not to hazard his own life by daily inspections and peregrinations, but have each of them report to him daily. This was the reason why it has been said that he conducted the defence from his bed.

Richelieu disembarked 15,000 men at Ciudadela on 18 April without incident. He was received well by the inhabitants, and pushed inland, but was held up at Ferrerias where the road entered a defile, and had been broken up at Blakeney's orders. The heavy siege train had to go back, and be taken by sea to Cala Mesquida on the eastern seaboard. His main force, however, reached the central village of Mercadal, where a small detachment turned north to take Fornells. The remainder arrived on the outskirts of Mahón three days later.

Here the Duc's progress lost momentum as he surveyed the vast St Philip's Fort. His maps were out of date, and it looked more formidable than he had expected.

The castle or fort which he now faced had first been built in the sixteenth century after the sacking of Mahón by Barbarossa, at the instigation of Emperor Charles V. Kane and Pettit had spent vast sums on its improvement according to the master fortress-builder Sebastien de Vauban, until it was now one of the most formidable fortresses in Europe. It was founded on mathematical principles, its general plan being a hexagonal star, enabling cross-fire to defend every point. Its redoubts, ravelins and other outworks were impressive, and many of its underground galleries, hewn out of the rock with incredible labour, had been mined against possible attack.

The inner enclosure of the fort was spacious, and buildings consisting of governor's house, chapel, guardroom and barracks surrounded a barrack square. These buildings had ramparts from which extensive views were afforded over sea and land in all directions. Easy access was provided by shallow steps with only a three-inch rise, so that laden mules and guns could be taken up. But what appeared above ground was only half the fort. The whole garrison could be housed underground. Here were living quarters, stores and arsenal all interconnected by underground passages, thus providing complete safety. Even guards going on and off duty could do so under cover. From the sea the fort was seen only as four large bastions surrounded by a deep ditch.

The Duc consequently made slower progress than he had hoped, and he and his aristocratic generals did not make a determined attack on the fort until after the arrival of Admiral Byng a month later. (It is said that it was during this period that a Mahón innkeeper invented a sauce for the Duc from eggs and oil, which he later introduced to France and the world as mayonnaise.)

When Byng reached Minorca's southern coast on 19 May, and hove to off the Isle of Aire, his loyal friend Augustus Hervey was not on the besieged island, but waiting for him at sea off Majorca, where he was being blockaded by two French ships. Their reunion was restrained but cordial. A first priority was to establish communications with the beleaguered garrison at Fort St Philip, where the Union flag—it was observed—still flew.

This proved difficult as they were exposed to enemy fire from La Mola opposite the fort, and sailing ships were at the mercy o the wind. Hervey offered to deliver a message from Byng to General Blakeney, and set off at dawn in the *Phoenix*, round the Isle of Aire, but the wind fell, and calm prevented a nearer approach. As he was probably just offshore from the modern resort of S'Algar, he was too far away from the fort to be observed. Contact had failed.

But in fact Robert Boyd, storekeeper in the fort for the previous sixteen years, had spotted the *Phoenix*, and begged Colonel Jeffries to allow him to row out immediately; but Blakeney unaccountably delayed his going till late afternoon. As a civilian Boyd may seem a curious person to have sent on such an important task, but Boyd was no ordinary man. In an age when—as was later said—officers were noblemen, and soldiers rogues, Boyd's subsequent career was unusual. Two years later he received a commission as lieutenant-colonel for his services to Minorca, and a distinguished military career followed, ending with the governorship of Gibraltar.

Boyd at last got away in a six-oared boat manned by ten sailors, but soon lost distance from Byng's fleet, owing to the direction of the wind. They had to return as dusk was falling, and their boat was fired on twice, although no one was injured.

To co-ordinate action contact was vital, but also to put ashore Lord Effingham, Lord Robert Bertie and his regiment, General Stuart and Colonel Cornwallis—all senior officers who would have been invaluable to Blakeney; but no further attempt at communication was made by either Byng or Blakeney.

THE BATTLE OF MINORCA

Although Byng had sighted the French fleet under Galissonnière the day before, there was at first no sign of it at dawn on 20 May; but at 7 am a sailor picked it up from a masthead. Byng reckoned it twelve miles offshore. He called his cruisers together at 10 am, and they 'tacked towards it and formed the line ahead'. Both fleets approached each other in extended line, parallel but from opposite directions, still many miles apart. The customary prelude to battle was a race to 'gain the weather gage', that is remain to windward of the enemy, which would give a vital advantage during the coming fight. It was an exercise in skilled seamanship, and Byng succeeded in this manoeuvre.

At this point Hervey, impetuous and spoiling for excitement, offered to sacrifice his ship the *Phoenix* as a fireship. He suggested that he and his crew abandon ship at the last moment, after it had been primed to go up in flames. Byng agreed, and Hervey filled the *Phoenix* with shavings, picked oakum dipped in resin, pitch, and mixed brimstone and gunpowder.

The British and French fleets each had twelve ships of the line and five frigates, and their armament was about equal. Naval battles in the days of sail were highly conventionalised in their manoeuvres, and the Battle of Minorca was no exception. The permitted movements of British ships, laid down in *Admiralty Fighting Instructions*, were almost inviolable. Byng himself had previously sat in judgement on courts-martial and sentenced fellow officers for infringement. He himself, by nature indecisive, was unlikely to deviate from the script, as the death penalty had just been introduced for doing so. Indeed pathetically—he went into battle holding a copy of the *Fighting Instructions* in his hand.

As the opposing fleets approached each other they converged, and proceeded to pass each other as in a dance. When Byng's leading ships were opposite Galissonnière's rear, Byng gave the order for each ship to tack and engage his opposite opponent. In this manoeuvre the British ships would wheel round to port, so that they were now sailing in the same direction as the enemy, but bearing down on them at an angle.

Among the first to engage was Byng's second-in-command Rear-Admiral West, now leading, who engaged his opponents at close quarters, at first too slowly and then so vigorously that the enemy ships opposite him were thrown out of line. At this point Byng took his fatal decision, and did not follow suit, failing to engage the enemy. His rear was thrown into disorder, and those in the van, left unsupported, suffered heavy damage from the broadsides of the French fleet as they sailed past. The French fleet, who had never sought a battle, then withdrew.

On the morning after the battle there was no sign of the enemy fleet, and Byng himself lay about ten leagues to the south of the island. He had lost contact with two of his ships—the *Intrepid* and the *Chesterfield*—during the night, and sent cruisers in search of them. When found the next day their masts were found to be badly damaged and the captain of the *Intrepid* had been lost. Byng called the inevitable Council of War on the 24th. In addition to three badly damaged ships, there had been a loss of forty-two killed and there were 168 wounded, with no hospital ship, and nowhere to put them.

The Council decided against further offensive action, and

recommended that the fleet proceed to Gibraltar forthwith with the wounded and to refit. Byng definitely meant to return to Minorca to renew the fight, as his dispatch written to the Admiralty at this stage shows: 'I hope we shall find stores to refit at Gibraltar, and if I have any reinforcement, will not lose a moment to seek the enemy again, and once more give him battle.' But the Admiralty, now fearing for their own lives, were determined to have Byng as a scapegoat, and censored this passage before its publication in the London *Gazette*.

Without any further attempt to contact Blakeney or inform him of his plans, Byng sailed from Minorca with his fleet the same afternoon.

Blakeney's first news of the departure of Byng's fleet was a *feu de joie* from the French lines on Cap Mola, opposite the fort. On land the enemy pressed the attack day and night but casualties were few on account of the underground passages of the fort.

On 27 June Richelieu personally led an assault, which appears to have been courageous and severe: 'Whole ranks fell around him, while the entire glacis was covered with dead and dying, some from the musketry and grapeshot poured on them from the front, others from the mines sprung beneath their feet, and at length he stood victorious on the summit of the Queen's Redoubt.' Colonel Jefferies was surrounded and taken prisoner, and Major Cunningham wounded by a bayonet in the arm. Thus the most important outwork and the assistance of Blakeney's two most important officers were lost. At the end of this bloody engagement a short truce was granted at Richelieu's request, to bury the dead and wounded on both sides.

The end of the siege was not far off. The outer defence works were now a mass of rubble, and the fort itself heavily damaged by the continuous bombardment. During the recent parley Richelieu had poured more men into the lodgements he had gained, and gained access to the underground passages leading to the very heart of the fort. A new and determined attack had been made from the sea, by scaling ladders. After a siege lasting seventy days, on 29 June 1756, Blakeney capitulated.

(*left*) Cala Mesquida, near Mahón, landing place of invasion forces under Duc de Richelieu in 1756, and again of Franco-Spanish forces in 1781. On the cliff is a defence tower; (*below*) medieval fortified farmhouse on Cavalleria peninsula in the north, used for defence against Moors and pirates

Page 106 Tower and gate of San Roque, Mahón, which is all that remains of the ancient city walls

The customary *chamade* (drum-beat signal) was sounded, and three of his officers came out of the fort and were conducted to Richelieu. The latter did not ask for unconditional surrender, and agreed to Blakeney's proposed terms. These showed that Blakeney was a tough and seasoned negotiator. In the Marshal's own words: 'Being desirous to show General Blakeney the regard due to the brave defence he has made, his troops were permitted to go, firelocks on their shoulders, drums beating, colours flying, 20 cartouches each man.' Ships were provided—against the surety of British hostages—for evacuation of British personnel and families, all of whom were permitted to take baggage and effects. Food for a twelve-day voyage to Gibraltar was provided. Sick and wounded who might be unable to travel were cared for.

The news of the French victory was brought to Louis XV at Compiègne, by Richelieu's son, de Fronsac, who had taken part in the expedition. It was the middle of the night, but the king was roused and there was general rejoicing. Mme de Pompadour had hoped the marshal would be defeated and thereby in disgrace, but now that he was a hero she was prepared to forgive and forget. There were parties and celebrations, and the Archbishop of Paris ordered a *Te Deum* to be sung in Notre Dame.

It was unfortunate that the first news the British Admiralty received of the defeat was from the same source. Both Galisson-nière's report of the Battle of Minorca and news of the capitulation reached the Duke of Newcastle and the king, via the Spanish ambassador in London. The king was angry, and the source of the news did nothing to assuage him. Indignation spread over England, and the guilty men of the administration were determined to distract attention from themselves. When Byng's own dispatches arrived they decided to arrest him on his return and bring him to trial. They accordingly 'edited' his account for publication, suppressing large passages which might be in Byng's favour or implicate themselves.

Effigies of the admiral were burnt by the populace throughout the country, while the more erudite wrote pamphlets which did not always side with the administration. Presently more substantial petitions against the government reached the king, one of which particularly shook the administration. It came from the Lord Mayor of the City of London, on behalf of the City Merchants. The reason for this disquiet was that it was the merchants who financed the country's wars, by acting as its moneylenders.

It took Byng twenty-six days to reach Gibraltar where he arrived on 19 June. There he was cheered to find Commodore Brodrick with a reinforcement of five ships for Minorca. It was a belated, albeit small offering from the Admiralty. Byng at once set about repairing his ships and taking on stores for an early return to Minorca.

His dismay can be imagined when the *Antelope* man-of-war arrived on 3 July with Admiral Hawke on board, bringing orders not only to succeed him in his command but to recall him to England. Gloom descended on Byng as he sat in his cabin and read;

> Sir,
> His Majesty having received an account that the squadron under your command and that of the French under Galissonnière came to an action off Mahón the 20th of last month; and that the French—though inferior in numbers—obliged you to retreat, I am obliged by the Lords Commissioners of the Admiralty to send you a letter of M. de Galissonnière to his Court, giving an account of the action; and to acquaint you that His Majesty is so much dissatisfied with your conduct, that he has ordered their Lordships to recall you and Mr. West, and to send Sir Edward Hawke and Rear-Admiral Saunders to command the squadron . . .

The Admiralty's action had been taken solely on an enemy report, and Byng replied briefly, expressing his surprise at being so 'ignominiously dismissed from his employment'. He sailed home a few days later, arriving at Plymouth in the *Antelope* on 26 July, expecting an apology for such summary treatment.

The reality was different. On stepping ashore he was arrested, placed in irons, and confined in a room without a bed. Orders were presently given to confine him in the Tower of London, but on the way there, his coach was halted by messengers, and he was told the Admiralty had changed its mind. He was sent back to Portsmouth, and next day despatched to the Royal Hospital at Greenwich (now the Royal Naval College).

At Greenwich he was put in a tiny attic room, with sentries placed at his door and on his stair. The Hospital Commandant was sadistic in his treatment, had bars put on his windows, and placed every obstacle he could in the preparation of his defence. Fortunately Augustus Hervey was back in England and threw himself wholeheartedly into the defence of his friend.

The trial opened at Portsmouth on board the *St George* on 28 December, and lasted for a month. It took the form of a court-martial and was legally constituted, but from the members selected there was little doubt what their verdict would be. He was tried under the 12th Article of War, which read as follows:

> Every person in the fleet, who, *through cowardice, negligence or dis-affection, shall in time of action, withdraw or keep back or not come into fight,* or engagement, or shall *not do his utmost* to take or destroy every ship when it shall be his duty to engage; and to assist all and every of His Majesty's ships, which it shall be his duty to assist and relieve; every such person, so offending, and be convicted thereof by the sentence of a court-martial, shall suffer death.— Act of George II.

A detailed account of the complicated trial falls outside the scope of this book. The vital clauses in the 12th Article are those italicised above. The verdict contained thirty-seven resolutions, some of which contradicted each other. He was cleared of cowardice and disaffection, but found guilty, and presumably of negligence (as this was the only other alternative) but the word was not used. The court added a recommendation for mercy, in which they contradicted their implied verdict of negligence, and expressed the opinion that he had only made an error of judgement, a much lesser offence which did not come into the 12th Article at all. To sum up, there was a gross mis-carriage of justice engineered by a hostile administration.

Sentence of death was promulgated on 27 January 1757, but was not carried out till 14 March, forty-six days later. The delay was due to qualms of conscience among his enemies, and the redoubled efforts of his friends, among whom Augustus Hervey was again to the fore. The king refused a reprieve. A stay of execution in Parliament also failed. In all this striving Hervey worked behind the scenes, and when all seemed lost the loyal captain visited Byng at Portsmouth to take his farewell, and plotted his escape. Hervey tells the cloak-and-dagger story in his diary:

> I set out for Portsmouth to see if there was not a possibility to help him to escape out of the hands of these bloodthirsters. I set out and lay at Ripley, where I left a set of horses. The next day I dined at Petersfield, and ordered four horses to be ready for me . . . night or day, determining to carry Mr. Byng to London as the surest place to get him off from, and wrote to my servant to have horses constantly saddled . . . and made him hire a Dutch fishing boat to send a 'servant' to France.

But all in vain: Byng was too closely guarded.

Before the curtain falls on the tragedy of Admiral Byng, a tribute came to him from an unusual quarter. On 19 January 1757 an oddly addressed package arrived at a London post office addressed to 'M. L'Amiral Byng'. It was from that champion of freedom and human rights, Voltaire, enclosing a letter of eulogy from the Duc de Richelieu himself. Its contents were made known to the king and government and it was withheld from Byng till after his court-martial.

Admiral Byng died bravely. The following is a contemporary account of his death which appeared in the *Evening Post*:

> On Monday, March 14th, 1757, all men-of-war at Spithead were ordered to send their boats and their captains and all their officers of each ship, accompanied by a party of marines under arms, to attend the execution of Mr. Byng. Accordingly they rowed from Spithead, and made the harbour a little after 11 o'clock, with the utmost difficulty and danger, it blowing prodigiously hard at N.W. by N., and the tide off ebb against them.

It was still more difficult to get so high as the *Monarque* lay, on board which ship the Admiral suffered ... There was a prodigious number of boats round the ship ... which kept all the others off. Not a soul was suffered to be aboard the *Monarque* except those belonging to it.

Mr. Byng, accompanied by a clergyman who attended him during his confinement, and two gentlemen of his relations, at about 12 came on the quarterdeck, when he threw his hat on the deck, kneeled on a cushion, tied a handkerchief over his eyes, and dropping another which he held in his hand as a signal, a volley from six marines was fired; five of whose bullets went through him, and he was no more. He died with great resolution and composure, not showing the least sign of timidity in the awful moment.

PLUS ÇA CHANGE

Minorca remained a French possession from 1756 for seven years till 1763, when it was again ceded to Britain under the Treaty of Paris at the end of the Seven Years War. As a measure of Britain's victory over France, Britain also gained Canada, Florida, numerous islands in the West Indies, and a free hand in India.

This short French occupation of Minorca was a happy one, for France was Catholic, and this eliminated many of the frictions under British rule. Their first governor was Count Cayetano de Lannion from Brittany, and Minorcans look upon him as one of the best governors they ever had. During this period the French built the little town of San Luis to house Breton sailors. Its little church is of this period, and bears the arms of Louis XV of France, after which the town is named.

The second British occupation of Minorca, which lasted for nineteen years, from 1763 to 1782, was less harmonious, owing to unsympathetic or self-seeking governors, and a fresh turn of the political wheel that brought new disasters to Britain. Once more there was neglect of the island's defences. The first British governor was General Johnston who served from 1763 till 1774, except for intervals when he was recalled to England for inquiry into his administration. Minorcans found him despotic, and unduly influenced by his wife, Lady Clare, who did not like the island. The Minorcan writer Verdaguer introduces them into his novel *Piedras y Viento* (Stones and Wind) about the island during this period. General Moystin, deputy-governor in 1771, is notable for having initiated the building of Georgetown, now known as Villa Carlos, and demolished the old suburb of San Felipe adjoining the fort. The military hospital on the King's Island in Port Mahón also dates from this year.

General John Murray succeeded Sir George Howard as governor in 1774, and was the last to hold the post during the second occupation. The appointment was evidently still considered important, as he was a distinguished soldier who had been one of Wolfe's brigadiers at the siege of Quebec, and had previously been governor of the new colony of Canada. He had a reputation for harshness.

Murray had further—familiar—cause for worry. Britain was feeling a strain on her sea communications brought about by her new far-flung empire, so that Minorca was again being starved of both men and supplies. In a personal letter to a friend at home at this time about a consignment of wine and grief at the death of his wife, he shows a deep distrust of the home administration. By 1778 Britain and France were again at war, and graver events cast their shadows.

The destinies of Minorca and Gibraltar became closely linked. In 1778 the four years' siege of Gibraltar began, and troops and supplies for Minorca had to pass through Gibraltar. There they were frequently retained by Gibraltar, who felt their own need was greater. In spite of this, Minorca gave much voluntary help to Gibraltar at this time. At night small supply ships from Minorca would break the blockade and slip into Gibraltar.

Minorcans and British even sent food parcels to their friends, until General Elliott, governor of the 'Rock' put a stop to it as he said 'at least a third of each vessel's cargo was employed for selfish purposes'. By 1781 Gibraltar's plight was so desperate that it was entirely dependent on Minorca for food and livestock, and Elliott and Murray secretly arranged convoys from Minorca to bring more massive supplies. France was fully aware of the source of all this help, and it was inevitable that she would put a stop to it by once more invading Minorca.

Unknown to Murray, a Spanish nobleman in the guise of a merchant had secretly visited Minorca in 1779 to gauge the likelihood of support from the Minorcan gentry in the event of a joint Franco-Spanish invasion, and his report had been satisfactory. And in 1781 Murray, having quickly overcome his grief at the loss of his wife, and married the daughter of the British consul in Majorca, now evacuated her and a child to Leghorn for safety, owing to his certainty of attack.

Diplomacy to save Minorca took the most bizarre twists at this time. It was suggested that Britain offer the island to Russia (retaining the right to use Port Mahón) if Catherine the Great would intervene, and bring about peace with France and Spain.

THE SIEGE OF MINORCA, 1781

France kept her preparations for attack secret, this time amassing her fleet and forces at distant Cadiz on the Atlantic. A joint Franco-Spanish fleet of fifty-two sail and sixty-three transports carrying 8,000 troops sailed from Cadiz on 2 July 1781, under command of the Duc de Crillon. The Marquis de Aviles landed a division at Ciudadela in the west, and a second division disembarked at Fornells in the north. The Duc himself chose the pink sands of Cala Mesquida. This landing was delayed by contrary winds, which gave Murray just time to withdraw his forces inside Fort St Philip. Crillon set up his headquarters at Cap Mola opposite the fort, at the mouth of the port.

When Murray checked his nominal rolls, he found he had 2,692 men of all categories, made up of 2,000 British and Hanoverian troops, including 400 invalids, who had been on the island for five years. He estimated that a fit garrison of 8,000 men was necessary to defend the fort, and had no illusions as to his plight.

Crillon, aware of his advantage in numbers, at first showed no inclination to join battle. In a kind of 'cold war' he offered

Murray a bribe of £1,000,000 and a lucrative commission in the French or Spanish service if—to avoid bloodshed—he surrendered immediately. This was curtly refused. The cold war continued, and conditions inside the fort are described in an 'on the spot' account which appeared in the *Annual Register* in 1781:

> The stores and magazines were amply furnished with every kind of salted provisions; with good bread, rice, peas, wine . . . all in such abundance as would have supported the garrison for a longer siege than actually occurred. But the single and fatal lack was fresh vegetables, which the island produced in abundance, and from which the garrison was now entirely cut off.

As a result scurvy soon broke out, with disastrous consequences. But Murray took the initiative, and sent a commando party in small boats with muffled oars from the fort to Cap Mola opposite, and not only raided Crillon's headquarters but occupied them for twenty-four hours. They returned to the fort safely the following night with 100 prisoners, including a lieutenant-colonel, three captains and four subalterns. Shortly afterwards a shell from the fort blew up a magazine on Cap Mola, killing many of the enemy. These early successes cheered the troops but could not affect the outcome. In February 1782, after a siege lasting eight months, the garrison surrendered.

In General Murray's final dispatch to Lord Hilborough he relates that his troops 'presented a pitiable sight' from scurvy and starvation, and that some sentries had died at their posts. All that were left were 600 decrepit soldiers, 200 seamen, and 120 of the artillery. As in 1756, the victors did not humiliate the vanquished. They 'marched from Fort St. Philip through the victorious Spanish and French armies who were drawn up in two lines, facing each other'. Overcome with emotion, the British troops declared they surrendered to God alone, and 'such was the distressing figures of our men'—wrote Lord Hilborough —'that many of the Spanish and French are said to have wept when they passed them'.

7   THE MAKINGS
OF MODERN MINORCA

SINCE 1802 Minorca has remained permanently Spanish.
With the exception of the sixteen years from 1782 till 1798,
she had not been her own master since the seventeenth
century.

For a last brief period from 1798 till 1802, there was a third
British occupation during the Napoleonic Wars, bringing
Minorcans within the orbit of yet another global conflict, but
protecting them from invasion by Napoleon's forces. This period
brought Minorcans into close contact with a Europe that was
moving away from the old ways. All these events greatly influenced the makings of modern Minorca.

A glance at the copy of a letter in the dispatch case of one of the
British commanders puts us into the context of contemporary
events:

To Sir William Hamilton   Ciudadela, Nov. 26th 1798

My dear Sir William,
    I am happy to tell you that the secret expedition . . . has been
attended with the greatest success . . . We must now look to the
preservation of this valuable conquest . . . The importance of so
excellent a Harbour as Mahón, must be sufficiently obvious . . .
    With my very best respects to Lady Hamilton
                                Thomas Graham

THE THIRD BRITISH OCCUPATION

The third British occupation of Minorca was led by two aristocratic Scots, Lieutenant-General Sir Charles Stuart, a scion of

115

the House of Bute, with Lord Lynedoch (Colonel Thomas Graham), laird of Balgowan in Perthshire, as his second-in-command. Both were brilliant soldiers. Graham, a man of wealth, did not join the army till he was forty-five years of age, and raised a battalion at his own expense. He quickly showed great courage and resource. Sir Arthur Bryant in *The Years of Endurance* refers to him as 'as natural a soldier as Cromwell', and considers that given a chance he would have 'won as great a name as Marlborough or Wellington'. Graham later founded the United Services Club in London, where his portrait can be seen.

Colonel Graham was holding a staff appointment in Ireland, when he heard that his regiment (then stationed at Gibraltar) was to form part of a force bound for a secret destination. Always keen for military adventure, he at once resigned his appointment, and set out for Gibraltar, where he learned that Minorca was the objective. During the voyage he wrote to his brother Lord Cathcart of his excitement, and sent him a list of the particular officers he wanted on his staff.

On 7 November 1798 a landing was made at the northern port of Addaya. The invasion fleet, consisting of two seventy-four-gun battleships, frigates and transports, under Commodore Duckworth, had intended to enter the Bay of Fornells, but this plan was abandoned because of high winds blowing out of the harbour. The main body of the fleet hove-to five miles off Fornells, and the troop transports under protection of the frigates *Argo*, *Aurora* and *Cormorant* went on to Addaya. As they entered this deep sheltered inlet they were immediately met by fire from shore batteries, but this opposition soon ceased on their receiving a few broadsides from the seventy-four-pounder British ships, and their gunners fled. The 28th Regiment of Highland troops under Colonel Paget were able to disembark by 11am, and went into action even before this operation was completed.

Writing a fortnight later from Ciudadela to his brother, Graham says: 'Half the troops were not landed when the enemy appeared. It was material to gain a height almost surrounded by a ravine before them, and this was effected by marching off those that were ready.'

Another contemporary account takes up the story:

> By six in the evening all the troops were landed, and immediately marched in pursuit of the enemy, who, by their knowledge of the roads, retreated faster than they could be followed. Some seamen being landed to drag the cannon, performed their work in a dark night, through the worst of roads. In the meantime, Commodore Duckworth had taken possession of the Bay of Fornells, and with the marines had garrisoned two of the forts at its entrance, which the enemy had evacuated.

Under cannon cover from the British ships, the invasion force drove off two divisions of Spanish troops, who were re-forming to retake the shore batteries. The Highland Scottish troops had been surprised to land on a rocky hillside covered with purple heather amid scenery so like that of their homeland, and were in great fettle.

The following day Stuart sent Graham with 600 troops 'along a broken and hazardous road which led round the hill of Monte Toro' to Mercadal at the centre of the island. This was achieved without British loss, the Spanish forces falling back to Ciudadela.

On the third day, a detachment of 300 troops under Colonel Paget marched east from Mercadal to Mahón, and compelled Fort St Philip to surrender. With admirable timing they removed booms across Port Mahón's entrance, which let the *Aurora* and *Centaur* from Fornells through. The remainder of the British invasion force headed west to Ciudadela, which surrendered without severe opposition on 15 November. The British force had numbered 3,000, and the Spaniards 3,600. Not a single British soldier was lost. It is a remarkable fact that the British found that the once formidable Fort St Philip had been deliberately destroyed by the Spanish themselves some years before, in case it should again be used against them.

NELSON AND MINORCA

Although Lady Hamilton lost no time in acclaiming the acquisition of Minorca, Nelson does not mention the island in his voluminous and almost daily correspondence, till six months later. The first time the name 'Minorca' appeared in a letter was on 12 May 1799, when he replied to Commodore Duckworth who had requested his presence: 'I am sending you 8, 9, or 10 ships of the line . . . for I cannot come to you.'

Nelson's spectacular victory at the Battle of the Nile in 1798 had given Britain supremacy at sea in the Mediterranean, and the occupation of Minorca a few months later was invaluable in maintaining it. But Nelson had returned after the battle to Naples with Lady Hamilton, and showed marked disinterest in the island, to the point of insubordination.

It is important to remember that in spite of his fame and his new peerage he was still a fairly junior rear-admiral, and only second-in-command in the Mediterranean. Early in June 1799 the commander-in-chief, Earl St Vincent, lay sick at Port Mahón, and shortly went home, handing over his command to Lord Keith, Nelson's senior by twelve years, but whom Nelson detested. Both St Vincent and Keith believed that the French might attempt to retake Minorca, and during July Keith twice ordered Nelson to send ships and men to Minorca, as he felt the fleet was too dispersed, and that Minorca was in danger.

Nelson thought otherwise, and twice disobeyed these orders, maintaining that his affairs with the king of Naples were more important. Nelson wrote at length to the Admiralty to justify this insubordination, maintaining that as the man on the spot he must decide for himself, but the Admiralty rebuked him.

Nelson's first recorded visit to Minorca was on 17 August 1799, when he wrote an account of events to the Duke of Clarence from Port Mahón—'where so much has required doing, that except to pay my visit to the General, and to the naval yard, I have not been out of the ship . . . I sail tomorrow for Palermo.' Lady Hamilton was apparently not with him.

Nelson visited Minorca on a second occasion from 12 to 18 October 1799, in the *Foudroyant*. The former naval chaplain to Earl St Vincent, the Reverend Cooper-Willyams, who was on the island at the time, describes his arrival: 'On the 12th the *Foudroyant*, bearing the flag of Lord Nelson, with some other ships of the line and frigates, arrived in the bay of Mahón. On paying my respects to the noble Admiral, I was very kindly received . . . the Admiral soon after sailed for Sicily.' If Lady Hamilton had accompanied him, this would have been mentioned.

Nelson remarks elsewhere on the discomforts of the captain's cabin in the *Foudroyant*, and it is possible that on this occasion he stayed at the Golden Farm above the port, as all tourists are told. This would have been a more inspiring and comfortable place for the literary composition with which he occupied his stay, for as he was now a hero of world fame, the editor of the London *News Chronicle* had asked for some notes for a biography.

As at Naples, social life at Port Mahón was not neglected, in spite of war. There were concerts and balls. At the latter we learn from Chaplain Willyams that the nun-like dresses of the Minorcan ladies 'formed a striking contrast to the more elegant and becoming appearance of the British ladies'. And 'in the evenings the band of the regiment played under the walls of the Lazaretto Island, on the margin of the bay. During the moonlight nights the effect was perfectly delightful: the evenings at this time were calm and serene, the water as smooth as glass, and over its surface small boats were constantly gliding . . .'

It is impossible to be certain that Lady Hamilton visited Minorca and the Golden Farm, which is disappointing for the tourist industry, but perhaps the legend serves equally well. Perhaps she could have done so in the early months of 1800, when Nelson was acting commander-in-chief during Lord Keith's temporary absence in England. Lady Hamilton returned with her husband and Nelson overland to England in June 1800. After that, she never left England.

THE MINORCANS IN 1800

The Reverend Cooper-Willyams, Master of Arts of Cambridge University, clearly knew the right people in high places. From the obscure vicarage of Exning in Suffolk, he became in 1798 domestic naval chaplain to the commander-in-chief of the Mediterranean, Admiral the Earl St Vincent, and was present with Nelson at the Battle of the Nile. He had varied gifts, and when not conducting burials at sea or instructing midshipmen in their religious catechism was a prolific writer of travel books, some of which he himself illustrated in colour.

In his book *A Voyage to the Mediterranean in His Majesty's Ship, Swiftsure*, published in 1802, he describes his stay in Minorca as the guest of General Stuart, and observes the island and its inhabitants with a journalist's curiosity. Of women's dress he writes:

> The habit of the Minorquin women is very remarkable and differs more from modern Europeans than any I have seen. At first landing, I mistook the women for nuns of the mendicant order. They are long waisted, and wear a piece of muslin and sometimes black crape under their chins, which, rising up on each side of the face, joins a handkerchief drawn tight across the forehead. Over this they have a large piece of muslin, which extends from the top of the head downwards like a cloak. Some of them wear mantles lappelled, and joined at the back with yellow ribband. Below this, their hair,—which is tied close to the head—is suffered to hang loose in form and quantity like a horse's tail.
>
> Their petticoats reach but a little below the knee. Of course they are remarkably attentive to the decorations of their legs and feet, which are universally, from the highest to the lowest, clad in clean white stockings and neat round-toed shoes.
>
> The Minorquin ladies, it is said, wish much to adopt the more elegant dress of the English, but either from some jealous fancy or a regard for the ancient costume of their country, the men will not permit it.

The men themselves, however, had adopted more modern fashions.

The author made several strenuous excursions by mule across the island, and in a coloured engraving in his book depicts a rural scene with Monte Toro in the background entitled 'Inhabitants of Minorca'. In the foreground are two country women, and a priest in long robes and a large beaver hat. But this picture is remarkable for its illustration of the method of making butter, which he describes in the text: 'a dairy woman is standing under a shed holding by two pegs in the wall to steady herself, while with one foot naked stamps in a tub of cream till it becomes butter'.

During this last British occupation, a temporary prosperity came to the island. Never had Minorcans seen so many ships in Port Mahón, nor so many troops encamped ashore. During the year 1800 over 2,000 ships had passed in and out of the harbour, and at one time over 25,000 troops were in camps around Mahón. This did not last after Minorca passed finally under Spanish rule by the Treaty of Amiens in 1802.

On 14 June the Spanish captain-general of Majorca, Don Juan Vives, landed in Ciudadela and hoisted the Spanish flag to the accompaniment of British artillery salutes. Two days later, at a very formal ceremony on the parade ground at Villa Carlos, the British governor Cleophane handed over the island, and revelry and rejoicing followed for some days.

Why Britain decided to relinquish Minorca after repeatedly fighting for it for a century is difficult to understand, and indeed there was almost a last-minute reversal of the decision. The handing over of Minorca to Spain was part of a 'package deal' with France, in which Britain agreed to relinquish Minorca, Elba and Malta if France would evacuate Egypt. But before the treaty was ratified, France had in fact done so. The British government rushed instructions to Cleophane not to hand over Minorca, but the ship bearing these dispatches arrived two days after the handing-over ceremony, and was further held up by the Spanish authorities.

With the departure of the British, the prosperity of the island waned, and when peace came there was a large influx of refugees and fugitives from France and Spain, who only served to increase the scarcity of food and necessities. As a result, many Minorcans during the nineteenth century sought release from penury by emigration.

A substantial emigration to Algeria took place in 1830, after the conquest of that country by France, the emigrants prospering until the independence of that country in the present century. Most of these resettled in France. Other immigrants went to California and Florida, and in the latter place descendants of Minorcans are still to be found.

The first emigration to Florida had taken place in 1768 during a previous period of economic depression in Minorca, during the second British occupation. Formerly Spanish, Florida had been taken over by the British at the end of the Seven Years War, and was thought to be a suitable location. A Scottish doctor— Andrew Turnbull—organised a group of 1,400 emigrants, who were sent out under the leadership of Francisco Pellier. A Minorcan colony was founded at New Smyrna, sixty miles south of the town of St Augustine, which had been founded in 1765. They worked for a time in indigo plantations, but were badly exploited. The 600 survivors settled in St Augustine.

In 1965 St Augustine city celebrated its 200th anniversary of its foundation. Some citizens in unusual costume attracted attention, and were asked whom they represented. They replied, 'We are Minorcans.' They were the descendants of the surviving 600.

AMERICA AND MINORCA

Between 1815 and 1826 Minorca entered a new and little-known period in her chequered history: a lasting link with America was forged, of which many Americans may be unaware. For eleven years Port Mahón was used as an American base, by the forerunner of the present American Sixth Fleet. The American Navy was stationed in the Mediterranean to protect her merchant shipping from the Barbary pirates who still infested the seas. At this late period, American crews and passengers were

Page 123 'The Street of the Bridge of the Castle', Mahón, an excellent vantage point to look down on the port, and on the site of the former Castle of Mahón

Page 124 (above left) Admiral Sir Thomas Allin; (above right) Lieutenant General
Stanhope; (below left) Sir Richard Kane; (below right) Captain Augustus Hervey

being seized as hostages, and even sold as slaves. The co-operation and good behaviour of the Deys of Tunis, Tripoli and Argel had been secured by payments of money, but Tripoli wanted more, and with some temerity had declared war on America in 1801.

Jefferson was for retaliatory naval action, but his hands were tied by Congress, and he settled for a naval blockade. It was not long before the Americans felt the need of a winter base. Two years later, successful aggressive action by Commodore Preble so raised American prestige among her enemies that Congress consented to further naval action against Tripoli, and America found herself fighting her first war in Europe.

Peace was made in 1805, but war broke out again in 1815, and it was in this year that Commodore John Shaw first entered Port Mahón with his Mediterranean fleet, and anchored in Cala Figuera (the former 'English Cove'). The Minorcan authorities were co-operative, and we learn from a contemporary diary that 'the Governor granted to the Americans the lease of the new Lazaretto for use as a hospital for their sick'. From that year till 1826 most American midshipmen received their naval training at Port Mahón.

It was no new experience for Minorcans to meet strangers—they had been doing so for nearly four thousand years—and they quickly settled down with their new guests. The additional trade and inflow of money was welcome, for Minorcans were still undergoing hard times. So great was poverty and distress on the island that starving Minorcans used to congregate on Cala Figuera in the port, hoping to beg some food from the American ships. The Americans were sympathetic, and undertook to feed many of them, by increasing their own ration allowance. By 1823 conditions had apparently improved, and the association between islanders and navy became more festive. The navy staged entertainments including balls, on shore, to which they invited the Mahónese. And on 22 February the birthday of George Washington was celebrated with much waving of flags and firing of salutes. Next day a great ball was held, and important people were entertained on board ship to lunch and dinner. America was showing that she too could organise a 'Fiesta'.

Admiral Farragut

There was a second notable American link. The days of sail passed, and on 27 December 1867 the city council of Ciudadela made elaborate preparations to welcome two American battleships, on one of which was the elderly Admiral Farragut—the first admiral of the American Navy.

The reason for the visit and the welcome was that the admiral was a Minorcan, a son of Jorge Farragut Mesquida who had emigrated to America towards the end of the eighteenth century. Admiral David Glasgow Farragut was born on 5 July 1801, near Knoxville, Tennessee. His father had emigrated from Ciudadela. His mother was Elizabeth Shine from North Carolina. On the early death of his mother he was adopted by David Porter, a friend of his father (who was often away at sea), with whose help he joined the American Navy at a very early age. We are told that before he was twelve, he had engaged in a skirmish with the British, but was refused promotion because of his age. Between 1815 and 1820 he served in the Mediterranean Squadron as a youth, but it is not known whether he visited his father's homeland. About this time he showed an aptitude for languages, the study of which he followed up at Yale University in 1826, and later at the Smithsonian Institution in Washington.

Fame came to him when he was over sixty years of age, with the outbreak of the American Civil War in 1861. He decided to support the Union, and became the hero of the campaign. By his bold action his squadron destroyed the defences at the mouth of the Mississippi, and he captured New Orleans. In this operation he destroyed eleven Confederate ships, and reduced Port Jackson and San Felipe. His successes were largely instrumental in the final victory for the Union forces. After these engagements, he was put in command of all the naval forces, and congratulated by President Lincoln in 1862, being promoted to the rank

126

of rear-admiral. In 1866 he was created by special ordinance, the first admiral of the American Navy.

The memory of the admiral is still cherished by Minorcans and Americans, and forms a lasting link between these two peoples. Indeed, each year they honour his memory together.

THE MOVE FROM THE LAND

As the nineteenth century advanced, there was an increasing movement of Minorcans away from the land, as it was no longer sufficiently productive to support a growing population. This led to further substantial emigration in the second half of the century, but in spite of this the population had risen between 1845 and 1887 to a record figure of 39,041, which represented a rise of over 8,000. This population was two and a half times the figure in Kane's census of 1723, but the island lacked a Kane to direct and advise.

The second reason for the move from the land was Minorca's own 'industrial revolution', which from small beginnings in 1860 gained momentum, and later embraced a series of industries. These ultimately did much to solve the island's agrarian problems, and are a major factor in Minorca's economy today. The first of these is the footwear industry, which owes its origin to Don Jeromino Cabrisas who had emigrated to Havana, where he built up a successful business, and then returned to Minorca. Seeing the plight of his countrymen, he chose several associates, and set up a factory in Ciudadela. The industry went on from strength to strength, exporting much of its production, and employing a large section of the population. During World War I, it received large contracts for the armies fighting in France.

A WIND OF CHANGE

At the beginning of the present century Minorca was a forgotten and unknown island, which nations no longer fought over. A few privileged visitors like Edward VII and the Kaiser called at

127

Port Mahón in their yachts—at different times—to enjoy the island's peace and privacy.

Minorcans went about their daily work in a leisurely fashion, indulging in their customary afternoon siestas, and the evening *tertulia* (social chat) in bar or by the quayside. The warm sun brought contentment, and the shuttered windows of their houses seemed to shut out the world as well as the wind. The more successful of them built small summer chalets by the sea, where they and their families spent as much time as possible in enjoyment of the still deserted and idyllic beaches. Thus Minorcans invented the cult of the weekend by the sea, before the habit became common in Europe or America. Alternatively, if the husband was a keen fisherman he would go alone, and occupy a convenient prehistoric cave at Cales Coves or Son Bou, to which he had fitted windows and a door.

The 'wind of change' came with the Spanish Civil War of 1936, which brought both terror and drama to Minorca. This event hurled Minorca headlong into the harsh and cruel realities of the first half of the twentieth century.

THE SPANISH CIVIL WAR

In the Spanish Civil War Minorcans showed their individuality as an island race, and declared for the Republicans, against the Franco (Nationalist) rebels. They maintained this position till the end of the war against all pressures.

There was immediate bloodshed in Minorca at the outbreak of war, for General Bosch who was commanding a detachment of troops on the island immediately declared for the rebels, and proclaimed a state of war. On 20 July Bosch's NCOs and men mutinied against their officers and declared for the Republicans, the civil population following suit. Later in the war, the general and his officers were shot in peninsular Spain without trial. In the disturbances, the cathedral at Ciudadela and the Sanctuary at the summit of Monte Toro were damaged. At Monte Toro the weapons used can still be seen with a plaque, inside the church.

The prehistoric caves found a new use, and became a hiding-place for 'wanted men'.

Towards the end of the Civil War, Minorca was almost alone in all Spain, in holding out against General Franco, and for one last time was to shake the corridors of power. Mussolini wanted to add Minorca to his Second Roman Empire, and waited with his troops in the wings at Majorca, no doubt feeling that the island and its port would be a suitable reward for his assistance.

Franco was equally determined that it should not fall into Italian hands, and approached the British Foreign Office for assistance in securing Minorca's submission to him. With the approach of World War II and Mussolini a potential enemy, Britain was willing to help.

In due course HMS *Devonshire* sailed into Mahón harbour with Franco's envoy on board to negotiate its surrender. The British naval commander acted as referee and host. A farcical international incident was just avoided when the Italian air force (based in Majorca) nearly bombed the *Devonshire* in Port Mahón by mistake.

8   TOWNS AND VILLAGES

W ITH the increasing migration of country people to urban centres, it is in the towns and villages that Minorcan life today can best be observed. All of these have their heritage in the past, their older features surviving and adapted for modern living, giving Minorcans a deep sense of history.

About 3km to the south-east of Mahón is the satellite town of Villa Carlos, built around the coves of Cala Fons and Cala Corp on Port Mahón, and 5km inland are the growing villages of San Luis and San Clemente.

The third town in size on the island is Alayor. There are three other small towns: Mercadal, Ferrerias and San Cristobal, all inland.

THE ROADS

All these places are connected by good roads, the road system consisting of a main one connecting Mahón and Ciudadela, and taking in all the other small towns on the way. From it subsidiary roads radiate north and south, taking one to Fornells and to various beaches, but many more surfaced roads are required to give access to all parts of the coast, the provision of which is being pursued with vigour.

The motor road from Mahón to Ciudadela passes through delightful undulating country, often climbing through pine forests, or descending gently into ravines with white farmhouses on hill-tops. The driver will find the traffic density pleasantly light. Proceeding from Mahón, one by-passes Alayor on its south side, and quickly reaches Mercadal at the foot of Monte Toro. Mercadal lies near the centre of the island, and is a kind of cross-roads. One can turn north to Fornells, or if bound for Ciudadela proceed direct to Ferrerias. Alternatively one can make a detour to the south to San Cristobal. (This latter route is more attractive.) From Ferrerias onwards the road is straighter and traverses flat country.

The Mahón–Ciudadela road is the traditional highway on the island. The present road was built in 1900 along substantially the same route as Kane's. The tourists' dream of a coastal road right round the island may well become a reality, but not many people know that the French constructed one for defence purposes during their occupation of Minorca from 1756 till 1763. It is shown as a track on some of the older maps, but no sign of it remains today, except for occasional crumbling dug-outs and gun emplacements.

The motorist entering Mahón or Ciudadela will find himself faced with immediate problems of car parking. Each is full of one-way streets, where local rules operate, and the unwary shopper returning to his car may well find a parking ticket on his windscreen, with a 10 per cent discount if he pays the fine within ten days. In place of parking meters, residents display in their cars what looks like a toy watch. On this they set the time of parking. The usual limit is an hour, and it is no use cheating; the warden makes regular patrols.

At Ciudadela, however, to show there is no ill-feeling a road sign greets the arriving traveller inscribed '*Bienvenidos*' ('Welcome'), and on leaving another: '*Feliz viaje*' ('Good journey').

MAHÓN

Mahón (pronounced with silent 'h' and accent on last syllable—Maón) is situated at the head of the port of the same name, on its south-western shore. The older part of the city is situated on high cliffs above the sea, so that from the quays it must be approached by steep roads or steps. The main thoroughfare from the quay is a noble carriageway with low balustrades which winds up directly into the town.

The view of the town from the quay or steamer is that of a foreign town, but at the top of the carriageway one enters what at first seems a busy small market town in Cornwall or Devon in England. This illusion is fostered by the narrow steep streets, and the prevalence of neo-classic British Georgian architecture, with fanlights, iron balustrades and sash windows. These last are not found anywhere else in Spain. After their first introduction by the British, Minorcan youths, accustomed to courting their *novias* (girl-friends) remotely through an iron grille, were in constant danger of decapitation as sash cords were not always used, and nicknamed them 'guillotines'.

The main shopping street, full of modern and well stocked shops, is called Hannover Street. It is a steep and narrow one-way street, fortunately often closed to motor traffic. A maze of narrow side streets branch off in all directions, without apparent planning, for the old town which is still the business centre of Mahón grew up within the original city walls of the sixteenth and seventeenth centuries. In 1740 the city walls were still more or less intact, but buildings had just begun to spread outside them. The only part of the walls remaining today is the sixteenth-century Gothic tower and bridge of San Roque, which is a prominent feature of the Plaza Bastion. It has two rectangular towers which contain rooms with loop-holes, and a gateway, formerly the En Severa Gate.

The necessarily confined space within which the old city was built gives it a friendly intimacy, and the concentration of historical buildings within a small area around the Plaza del General Franco—adapted and adorned for modern use—give a sense of continuity in the city's life. During the Napoleonic Wars, the Plaza was known to the British as the Grand Parade, and Chaplain Willyams has depicted it in a coloured engraving. This shows a group of British officers in dashing uniforms standing in the middle of it enjoying a leisurely conversation, and a couple of red-coat guards at the military headquarters nearby. The background of buildings is identical to that today; only the actors and props have changed. It is now a busy thoroughfare with a car park.

On the right of the Plaza is Mahón's parish church, the church of Santa Maria, whose lofty tower can be seen from the port. Founded by Alphonso III of Aragon as a pious act in 1287 after his conquest of the island, it was rebuilt in 1748, and blessed in 1772 during the British governorship of General Johnston. The new architecture was neo-classical. The church has one nave, and a famous monumental pipe-organ, which attracts organists of international renown. Facing the onlooker and beyond the church, the eye is at once attracted by the handsome City Hall which was built in 1613 and refashioned in 1778. The clock in its tower was brought from England by Sir Richard Kane, and here he occupied the governor's ceremonial chair on official occasions. Today, as the city's Council Chambers, it performs a similar function. The building is of striking architecture, of a transitional type between Renaissance and neo-classical. It has three arches and a *loggia* in front, at first-floor level, with a central exterior stairway leading up to it. Apart from a basement which contains a permanent exhibition of local industries (jewellery, silver and leather), the building therefore has only one main floor. One enters the vestibule by a central doorway at the top of the stairs.

Embedded in the wall of the right *loggia* before entering is an ancient coat-of-arms, carved in stone, of the city of Mahón, and in the vestibule itself are two inscribed blocks of stone, both of historical interest and one of great antiquity. The one on the left records the municipal status given to Magón (Mahón) by the Romans, while that on the right is inscribed with the arms of the former St Philip's Fort, being all that remains of it today. This was preserved in the museum in Majorca till 1972, when it was returned to Mahón through the good offices of the provincial governor. Beyond the vestibule is the old British 'throne room' or reception hall, now the Council Chambers, with a gallery of notable Minorcans dating from 1858. The square pilastered tower of the City Hall is crowned by a wrought-iron cupola.

Plaza de la Conquista

Turning to the right, in front of the City Hall, one enters a smaller square—the Plaza de la Conquista—which has a monument in its centre commemorating the conquest of the island by Alphonso III of Aragon—clearly the island's hero. In this dignified square, which is at the back of the church of Santa Maria, is housed the Casa de Cultura, a first-class museum and reference library. It stands on the original site of the old castle of Mahón, and close by is a narrow lane with the romantic name of Calle del Puente del Castillo ('the Street of the Bridge of the Castle').

On the far side of the square, one sees an archway leading into a short lane with tall Georgian houses on each side. This is one of Mahón's most photographed (or sketched) views. At the end of this cul de sac is a parapet, over which one gets a splendid view of the port far below.

Retracing one's steps into the Plaza del General Franco, it is but a short walk into the street called 'Isabel II'. This street is notable for its fine examples of neo-classical town houses with wrought-iron balconies, but one's attention will be drawn to a military sentry on duty at the gateway of a large courtyard on the right. This is the military governor's palace: a rambling white building in the old colonial style, also used by Kane.

Just past it is the narrow arched lane—Es Pont d'es General—believed to be the oldest surviving Moorish street in Mahón, although some date it from the fourteenth century. A little farther on one comes to the church of St Francis, whose cloisters have recently been converted to a cultural centre.

Shops

The shops in the main streets of the old town are modern and well-stocked with all the goods one expects in a prosperous, industrialised Western state. Prices are relatively high compared with Britain, especially for food. The most opulent shop-fronts are those of the estate agents. A recent attractive innovation is the pedestrian shopping precinct of Calle General Goded, with its gay coloured tiles and stone tubs of plants. All provision shops sell frozen foods, and the supermarket self-service system is common. Anything can be bought from cars to cakes. The latter deserve special mention for local specialities, either to visit or avoid, depending on how one views such matters. In addition there is a large covered market in what were previously the cloisters of a monastery in the Plaza del Carmen. Here every variety of vegetable, fruit, meat and poultry can be bought.

Minorcan shop assistants are extremely courteous, but by foreign standards could be considered slow. This should not be judged a fault, but taken as a reminder that in Minorca haste and bustle are sins and futilities to be avoided. The wrapping up of one's purchase is a ritual to which much care and time is devoted.

In the side streets there are few shop windows or shop signs, and there seem to be no shops here at all. But behind the door of what looks like a private house is a small grocer's or bakery. In the latter one makes one's choice from a variety of small loaves on a tray, straight from a great oven. As one does so, an occasional old woman enters with a pot of stew to be cooked in the glowing embers. In the dark recesses of the room is a pile of pine branches for fuel. It is only a few yards from the travel agents and the banks, but the procuring of bread is a daily ritual in Minorca, and the scene could be medieval.

All shops close at 1.30pm because of the customary siesta, re-opening about 4.30pm and staying open till 8. The streets are deserted in the afternoons, and gay and brilliantly lit in the evenings. Shop assistants have certain evenings off, and longer periods at the weekends during the summer months—'for recreational purposes', namely, the beaches.

Outside the walls

When Mahón spilled outside its old town walls, it was limited to the north and east by the sea, and had of necessity to expand inland towards the south and west. This newer, flatter and more spacious part of the city includes the great Square or Explanada, which is laid out artistically with palm trees, shrubs, children's playground, bandstand, illuminated fountains, and car park—and is an attractive public park. Most of the dignified buildings bordering it date from the late eighteenth or early nineteenth centuries. Its east side is taken up with gay street café-bars, restaurants, and coach stops for coaches from all parts of the island. On the south side is a taxi-rank. From the Explanada wide roads radiate to San Luis, to the international airport and to Ciudadela. This whole area presents a busy animated scene.

Recently a number of less attractive concrete blocks of flats and shops have been built on the outskirts of this section of Mahón. Beyond these is the large Military Hospital which replaced that of the Isla del Rey in the port in 1964, and a vast, extremely well laid out industrial complex (known as the 'Industrial Polygon') which concentrates the island's industries in modern automated factories. On the same road the airport is a further 4km away, on the road to the village of San Clemente.

Limited extension of Mahón's boundaries is also taking place in the east, along the main road towards the satellite town of Villa Carlos. The bulldozers are busy removing soft limestone cliffs. From this point it is a short car run to Port Mahón Hotel, the town's only four-star hotel, where it is pleasant to stop for a drink and to admire the view of the port.

VILLA CARLOS

Villa Carlos (nowadays sometimes written 'Villacarlos') is situated on the little bays of Cala Fons and Cala Corp on the southern shores of Port Mahón and is 3km from Mahón. It has the distinction of being the most easterly town in Spain. Like Mahón it is steeped in history, but has in recent years blossomed into a thriving holiday resort with three modern hotels with swimming pools. It has a picturesque, small water-front, with cafés, bars and discothèques, some in caves.

If Mahón's development was haphazard, Villa Carlos is an

excellent example of eighteenth-century town-planning, the design of its streets being the now common one based on the right-angle or grid pattern. The reason is that it was a purpose-built town designed by the British to house military personnel and their families from the nearby garrison of Fort St Philip. The British called their new cantonment Georgetown after George III, and when Britain lost Minorca to the Spanish in 1782 it was renamed Villa Real de Son Carlos, which became shortened to its present-day name of Villa Carlos. It still has a Stuart Street and a Victory Street, and a spacious barrack square known today as the Champ de Mars, in British colonial style, that could have come straight out of New England. Its barracks are still in use by Spanish military and police departments, and the Georgian building with its clock-tower is the present Municipal Chambers. The armorial bearings of the town still include the figure of St George of England.

This account of a truly unique town would be incomplete without relating the still stranger story of its predecessor, St Philip's Town, which stood nearby and has now completely vanished.

As early as 1554, when building of the first Fort St Philip began under the engineer Calvi, the workmen lived in a village they built near by, which grew to 3,000 by 1685, and became known as Felipet. Like most pioneer settlements it had a reputation for lawlessness, and when the British started extending and strengthening the fort in 1713 they demolished Felipet, and built a small town about 500m farther back which was at first called Arrabel Vella ('the suburb'). This soon spanned the whole neck of the peninsula to the south of the fort, as is shown on contemporary maps, and was named St Philip's Town. This housed the British garrison and their families until just before the French attack in 1756, when it was realised that it would give excellent cover for an enemy attacking the fort, and was therefore partly demolished. It was not, however, completely razed to the ground till 1774, in the middle years of the second British occupation, when Georgetown was built in its place.

SAN LUIS

From Villa Carlos it is but a few kilometres' drive to the little French town of San Luis, built during the French occupation that followed on the Byng disaster in 1756. One can also approach San Luis by the main road from Mahón, leaving it by the Esplanade. On this road one passes on the right the small former airport, now Minorca's private flying club. San Luis shines white in the brilliant sunlight, and has several equally white villages around it. The remains of its many windmills (used to pump water) indicate that it had previously been a populated agricultural area, as also do its defence towers, a notable one being at Binifadet. For such a very small town, it has a very big dual carriageway, gay with flowers on the dividing islands. The planners are clearly looking to the future.

SAN CLEMENTE

San Clemente has good prospects for the future as it is close to the international airport and on the way to a number of important tourist developments, which include Binixeica, and Cala'n Porter. It grew from a tiny group of peasant dwellings in the fourteenth century known as Musupta, a name which still appears on a number of outlying houses; but it was first occupied at a much earlier period. Near by is the prehistoric talayot of Torelló, and the remains of a Christian basilica dating from Roman times.

ALAYOR

Alayor, Minorca's third town in size (the population is a little over 5,000), is built spectacularly on a hill. The hill is crowned by its parish church of Santa Eulalia, and its white buildings gather round it on the slopes. With Monte Toro rising behind in the distance, it is an impressive sight when approached from the south via Torralba. Alayor is said to have been founded in

138

1304 by Jaime II of Majorca, but the prefix 'al' in its name suggests Moorish origin. It has, however, been a centre of population for much longer, as its relics of Roman roads and surrounding prehistoric villages indicate. The church of Santa Eulalia was built towards the end of the seventeenth century, and has an attractive interior. If one climbs the narrow street beyond to the summit of the hill, there are fine views of the countryside, with low hills to the north.

Alayor is a municipality, and the local government administrative centre for the *termino* (or district) of Alayor, which includes Cala'n Porter. Its chief industry is shoemaking, which is of a very high standard, largely carried on as a cottage industry. Like the other small towns in Minorca, it has a lively community life, with its art exhibitions, sports and fiesta days, even its chess tournaments (in spite of the popularity of television). Just outside Alayor, on the road leading to the west, is a pleasant little club with tennis courts, swimming pool and restaurant, which the visitor may use for a modest payment. Alayor has one more claim to our notice. Its inhabitants are noted for being musical, and hold a Minorcan Song Festival each year, which also attracts outside talent. This is broadcast on national radio channels.

MERCADAL

Mercadal lies at the centre of the island, under the shadow of Monte Toro. Although roads radiate from it to various parts of the island, it is a quiet and almost sleepy village. Much of the finest agricultural land is around Mercadal, so that farming is a major industry. Shoes and furniture are also made.

SAN CRISTOBAL

San Cristobal is a pleasant village on high ground, through which one will pass on the way to Santo Tomas beach, in the south. It was founded in 1769 and grew around a hermitage. To the archaeological student the village and surroundings are notable for having the greatest density of megalithic remains on the island: five to the square kilometre. Some of these are of exceptional interest and will be noted in the chapter describing excursions. Francisco Camps, a noted Minorcan historian and student of local folklore, was born here. Although San Cristobal is only a village, it is known locally as Mitjorn Gran, which means 'the large town to the south'.

FERRERIAS

Ferrerias, on the main road to Ciudadela, is situated in a ravine, sheltered from the north by the hill of S'Enclusa, and is the highest town on the island. It is expanding, but is not a particularly attractive town; it is proud of the wonderful beaches within its *termino*, including Santa Galdana. The town's main industry, apart from farming (some of it run on co-operative lines), is mainly the manufacture of high-quality furniture.

CIUDADELA

Ciudadela, like Mahón, stands on a cliff at the head of a port, but there the resemblance between the towns ends. Its port is a narrow and short inlet (1,100m in length), with steep sides prone to violent storms and even small tidal waves. (The water-level has been known to suddenly rise more than two metres.) In the town itself there is not a single building to remind one of the British. It is a cathedral city and the ecclesiastical headquarters of the island, with a population of a little over 12,000. A local saying goes: 'Mahón may have more people, but Ciudadela has more souls.' It has mellow, ancient palaces and arcaded streets (*ses voltes*), and is typically Moorish and Spanish in character, just as Mahón was British. But Ciudadela does not live in the past, being the centre of the shoemaking industry, and a business centre with excellent shops. A visit to Ciudadela makes a pleasant change.

Its port has regular sea communication by steamer with

Page 141   Hannover Street, Mahón: usually this is a busy shopping street, but this photograph was taken during the afternoon siesta

Page 142   (above) View of Ciudadela from its port, showing the cathedral against the skyline; (below) Fornells, a fishing village in the north

Majorca—with Alcudia (3 hours) and with Palma (8 hours), and excursions can be made in the summer months. Private yachts also use the port at that time. It is a steep descent to the port, where the Yacht Club is situated, and the usual fishing craft and café bars. Without descending to the port one can get an excellent view of it from Borne Square, also called the Plaza Generalissimo, which is one of the main features of the town.

The old part of Ciudadela, which was completely walled up to the mid-eighteenth century, is still the heart of the city's life. A large road-sign on the outskirts informs us that we are approaching a town of 'national tourist interest', and we enter its centre by crossing traffic lights into the little Plaza of Alfonso III, with its gay fountain and open-air cafés. Here, as one enters the narrow street called Virgen Carmen into its shopping area, stood the Mahón Gate, one of five gates, none of which now survive. The former landward walls followed the present course of the wide boulevards of José Antonio, Conquistador and Negrete which one has just crossed. The only remaining part of the walls is that overlooking the port itself. Passing the cathedral on the right, and the shady Moorish arches in the shopping street, it is best to proceed direct to Borne Square to park one's car, and retrace one's steps on foot.

Borne Square

The spacious Borne Square is pleasantly free of traffic. 'Borne' means 'palisade', and indicates that it was once used for knightly equestrian contests and jousting in the Middle Ages. In its centre is a tall obelisk raised by the citizens to commemorate their heroic defence against Turkish invaders, under the command of the renegade Admiral Mustapha Piali in 1558.

The Municipal City Hall on the west side of the square is the former Moorish *Alcazar* or Governor's Palace, which has had many tenants. A residence of the Moorish governors in the Middle Ages, and later of senior British military officers, it was restored and put to its present use early in the present century. It has a fine Gothic Hall with panelled ceiling and houses the

Municipal Museum. Among the portraits is one of the American-Minorcan Admiral Farragut. Facing the hall and to its right, one looks down perpendicularly over the ramparts of the old city wall to the port far below. To its left access can still be gained to the port by a steep flight of steps (formerly through a postern gate) and known as La Cuesta del Mar. On the east side of the square is the eighteenth-century palace of the Count of Torre Saura, which has a dignified and pleasing exterior. It is privately owned and not open to the public. It has an inner courtyard with ivy-covered walls which opens into noble rooms with fine pictures and furniture, with a throne-room. The south side of the square opens into modern, wide residential boulevardes and shady squares, and leads also towards the sea.

The cathedral and seignorial palaces

Retracing one's steps on foot through the white arcaded main shopping street, one enters the small square of Pius II, and stops on the left at the Gothic cathedral, which dates from the fourteenth century, and was built on the site of a mosque, small parts of which are incorporated in the present building. Alterations and additions have taken place from time to time but do not detract from its beauty. Some of the domes were rebuilt in 1626, and the main neo-classical façade in 1814. The Aragon and Ciudadela coats-of-arms appear above one of the doors. The interior is pleasing. It has a single nave in ogival Catalan style, and an apse in the shape of a pentagon, in which there is a choir with Gothic benches. It has three chapels in the Renaissance style. The cathedral was badly damaged in the Spanish Civil War, and has since been restored.

Two notable buildings stand close to the cathedral, the Olivar Palace opposite its main door, and the Bishop's Palace. The spacious rooms of the Olivar Palace house art collections and private archives. It has a library, and coin and archaeological collections. The Bishop's Palace is neo-classical, with an attractive patio with an arcaded gallery in Italian Renaissance style. Most of Ciudadela's palaces are in the Baroque style of the eighteenth century, but have been added to from time to time. In the Calle Santissimo is a second palace, belonging to the Saura family, which has a beautiful original Baroque façade.

The city's numerous palaces came to be built as a result of the increasing prosperity of the island's new aristocracy from the wool trade in the seventeenth century. The foundations of this aristocracy were laid in 1287 when, at the time of his conquest, Alphonso III of Aragon divided the lands of Minorca among his generals and favourites. Alphonso was both haphazard and generous in his gifts; a contemporary document states that he gave away whatever he was asked for, and earned the name of 'Alphonso the Liberal'. The recipients became known as *Caballeros*. Twenty-five years later his successor Jaime II of Majorca rationalised this state of affairs, and effected a redistribution of lands. More important, he introduced a wise system of inheritance (known as *hereu*), which in substance remains today. While large farms usually passed to elder sons, the important clause was that which prevented divided inheritance, and their breaking up into small units.

At the beginning of the sixteenth century the *Caballeros* began to leave their country homes and settled in Ciudadela, though they were still comparatively poor as a result of the perennial disasters of drought, famine and disease. There life continued to be austere for a time, but when the Spanish craving for noble titles spread to Minorca in the early seventeenth century, richer merchants began to marry into the local aristocracy, and from this time onwards the building of the palaces began.

Other notable palaces are the Martorell Palace of the Duke of Almenara Alta, that of the Baron of Lluriach (one of the oldest titles in the island), and the palace of the Marquis of Menas Albas. These have high-sounding names, and unfortunately their doors are closed. Most of them are characterised by great marble staircases, moulded ceilings and large carved double doors leading into drawing-rooms often furnished with Chippendale and Queen Anne furniture. Some have secluded courtyard gardens.

Today, thanks to the laws of Jaime II, a few large proprietors still own about half the island. In this respect little has changed since the Middle Ages, but it does not mean that the present big proprietors are the descendants of Alphonso's favourites. Only the Count of Torre Saura could count as such, his family name of Squella appearing in the records of the time. The present-day Minorcan aristocracy dates mainly from the nineteenth century.

9   *MINORCA TODAY*

ADMINISTRATIVELY, Minorca today forms part of the Province of the Balearic Islands, which is one of the fifty provinces of Spain. As such it comes under the jurisdiction of a provincial governor, appointed by the central government and responsible to the Minister of the Interior.

The provincial capital is at Palma in Majorca but, apart from official connections, Minorcans feel that for ethnic and historical reasons they have more kinship with Barcelona and Catalonia on the peninsula.

The governor effectively controls the life of the province, and is responsible for public order through the civil guard (police), and in emergency the army. Minorca is sufficiently important to have a deputy civil governor who is resident on the island, with his headquarters in the Plaza Miranda (Delegación Gobierno Civil), Mahón.

As Minorca could again be strategically important in a national emergency, it also has a military governor, whose residence and headquarters (Gobierno Militar) are in the Calle Isobel II in Mahón. He has no civil jurisdiction in time of peace, except in so far as he advises on military matters.

The civil governor has at his disposal as a consultative body a provincial council or assembly, which has a very wide representation. In addition to local government representatives drawn from municipal bodies, there are also members drawn from business, cultural and professional interests. The provincial council can be suspended if politically disaffected—a measure often adopted in the past by Britain during civil unrest in India—and direct rule assumed by the governor.

Alcaldes (mayors) of municipalities with populations of over 10,000 are appointed by the government, thus ensuring a high calibre of incumbent. The governor appoints mayors in the smaller towns. It is not until we reach members of the municipal councils that the democratic popular vote operates. Here too, there is similar wide representation of interests, divided among the vacancies.

SOCIAL SERVICES

Apart from the modern military hospital on the outskirts of Mahón, the island has three civilian hospitals. These are the municipal hospitals at Ciudadela and Mahón. Mahón has an additional hospital for insured private patients known as the Residencia Sanitaria. Minorcan doctors are trained to a high standard, and routine major surgery is carried out at these hospitals. Advanced specialist surgery is carried out at Barcelona, where some branches (especially ophthalmology) have a world-wide reputation.

Minorcans share in the provisions of a state medical service, which is obligatory to lower-paid workers and their dependants, but is not as comprehensive as the British National Health Service. It is known as SOE, and is administered by a National Security Institute, which works in collaboration with mutual insurance societies and private agencies.

Sickness benefits are approximately 75 per cent of basic wages and dependant allowances, for thirty-nine weeks in a year. Hospitalisation and medicines in hospital are free up to twelve weeks. These limitations are clearly due to financial reasons. Many workers obtain longer benefit by contributing to one of the mutual societies. Minorcans who because of a high income fall outside the state scheme also insure privately. This covers hospital treatment, but not medicines.

Maternity benefits are comparatively generous, except for pre-natal care, which does not operate until the sixth month of pregnancy. However, it includes treatment in hospital and 75

148

per cent of earnings for six weeks before and for six weeks after birth.

General practitioner service

This differs from the British practice, and is linked with a hospital outpatient consulting service. Contributors are allotted to hospital outpatient clinics, where they are seen by the general practitioner on whose list they have been placed.

The proportion of doctors to population compares favourably with other European countries and with America. In Spain there is, on average, one doctor per 829 persons, in England one per 1,104 persons, and in the United States one per 765 persons. (These figures are for 1960.)

Social security payments

National insurance is compulsory, and covers the following contingencies: temporary absence from work, accidents, assistance to dependants, permanent incapacity, widows' and old-age pensions. The last are jointly contributed by employee and employer, and are considerable, employees paying 42 per cent and employer 48 per cent (figures from *Europa Yearbook*, 1962).

TRADE AND INDUSTRIAL RELATIONS

Minorca has substantial exports of cheese, beef and footwear, and consequently shares with peninsular Spain in a preferential trade agreement with Common Market countries which was concluded in 1970. In 1971 Spain's exports to these countries increased by 28 per cent, and in 1972 the export–import trade balance between Spain and the United Kingdom was in Spain's favour. The industrial economy of Minorca is in an equally healthy state.

Trade unions in Minorca (as in Spain generally) have a different connotation to those in Western democratic countries. They are state-controlled, and their members comprise representatives from both sides of the shop floor—employers and employees—in addition to technical experts.

They concern themselves mainly with working conditions, improving pay and paid holidays. Examples of measures achieved have been child allowances and loans on marriage. Their widely based membership makes them well fitted for the consideration and settlement of disputes and wage claims. It goes without saying that strikes are illegal, but the worker nevertheless has considerable rights, and cannot be dismissed without right of a tribunal. (The same applies to a domestic servant.)

Minorca shows few signs of a totalitarian state. It has fewer stresses and inequalities than peninsular Spain.

EDUCATION

Minorcans today, with increasing international contacts, place a high value on the importance of education. They also equate education with culture. Schools conform to the general Spanish pattern, and are either state-controlled or private. Primary state education from the ages of six to fourteen takes place in the state primary schools and is free. Children are, however, accepted from the age of four, which is in effect analogous to the trend towards nursery schools in other Western countries, but for the most part the schools lack any special nursery facilities. In Minorca this early schooling is freely taken advantage of. In many villages there are one-teacher schools. School buses also transport country children to central schools, as in England.

At the age of ten, children either pass to a state secondary school or continue advanced primary education for another four years, until the age of fourteen. If they have been late developers these then have another chance of secondary education.

State secondary education is free, although the cost of books and other expenses can be high and is met by parents. Secondary-school places are, however, often inadequate in the state schools, and private schools make up for lack of them. At secondary schools pupils attend a six-year course with annual examinations, leading to the final *Bachillerato*, which is the equivalent of the General Certificate of Education (O- and A-levels) in Britain. Further examinations are necessary for university entrance at Barcelona and elsewhere. An increasing number of senior pupils at Mahón and Ciudadela study for their *Bachillerato* or university entrance at college evening classes. At the present time steps are being taken to increase these facilities, and a Balearic university is mooted.

For Minorcan children school usually begins at 8 am and goes on till 6 pm, except for the younger children. This includes a half-hour morning break and two hours for lunch and rest. They have two free afternoons a week of which one is a Saturday. Football, basketball and running sports are organised. Summer holidays are long and, except for the youngest pupils, extend throughout the hot summer months from July until the end of September. In addition to three weeks at Easter and Christmas there are fiestas.

Higher education of youths is often interrupted by national military service, which lasts for three years. Girls do compulsory social work at social centres and, just to encourage them, they are not allowed driving licences or passports for foreign travel until they have completed it.

English is now taught as a second language in schools and, owing to tourism, adult classes are now also common. With the opening of St George's English School for general education, the knowledge of English is spreading.

INDUSTRIES

Minorca is fortunate in having three industries: agriculture, manufactures and tourism.

Agriculture

We have seen when considering the makings of modern Minorca that there was a move away from the land in the nineteenth and early twentieth centuries, due mainly to the growth of the footwear industry. This fall in the rural population accelerated in the ten years from 1955 to 1965, for similar reasons, and now only about 10 per cent still live off the land. This, however, has provided the necessary stimulus to channel farming into new ways, which have proved extremely successful.

Knowledge of the island's geology has been used to assess the potential of individual soils. The island's two geological zones—south and north—known traditionally by the Minorcan countryman as Migjorn ('Land of the south wind') and Tramontana ('Land of the north wind'), differ agriculturally. As the south is essentially a limestone plateau, the soil is relatively light and retains the warmth of the sun. Although it is excessively stony, it has been favoured from time immemorial by Minorcan farmers.

By contrast much of the soil in the north has a silica content, which makes it less absorbent of moisture and warmth, and its fertility is more variable, owing to the overlay of different geological strata. In less sheltered parts the fury of the *tramontana* causes erosion, and the pattern of dividing-walls found in the south is absent. Lagoons, which were caused by poor drainage and stagnant water, at one time made the north malarial, and its unhealthiness probably contributed to its late development. Today, with modern techniques, some of the largest and most productive farms are in the north.

In achieving this, mechanisation has helped the farmer to till his land with fewer labourers. The Roman plough drawn by oxen has survived into the present century—and is still occasionally seen—for its shallow furrow was all that was possible in the thin, stony soil. The modern rotovator used in orchards and market gardening in other countries was the answer, and on the larger fields in the north tractors became increasingly common. Although many farms in Minorca are run either by their owners or by tenant farmers, in recent years, some co-operative schemes have been introduced with official backing, with a view to cutting costs.

Although Minorcan farmers still grow wheat, barley, oats, potatoes and vegetables, they have now turned to extensive cattle-rearing for milk, cheese and export of beef. The visitor often sees healthy Friesian cattle in the green irrigated fields. These now number 25,000. Sheep are also intensively reared. Scientific selection of cattle stock and artificial insemination are carried out, and 200,000 tons of *hedysarum coronarium* are grown and stored in silos for fodder. This is the Italian sainfoin of the vetch family, first introduced by the British in the eighteenth century, and still called 'enclova' by Minorcans on account of its profusion of red clover-like flowers.

In place of the numerous windmills and ancient Persian-style water-wheels propelled by oxen, increased irrigation and sinking of wells have been encouraged by the National Settlement Institute. This has done much to overcome the problems of drought, which previously caused the deaths of thousands of livestock and famine. Hundreds of sprinklers distribute the water from artesian wells, which are tapped by mechanical means.

This adoption of animal husbandry is in some ways a return to the pattern of farming in early times. It will be remembered that one of the ancient names for the island was Meloussa—the island of cattle—and we have seen that in the Middle Ages much of the wealth of the large farms came from the production of wool.

Manufactures

The three main manufactured products are cheese, footwear and costume jewellery. Cheese production is largely carried out in modern automated factories, using the milk from a large proportion of the island's cattle. However, traditional full cream cheese is still produced on the farms. Eighty per cent of the factory-made cheese is exported to the Spanish peninsula where it is famous, and the amount increases annually. One factory producing a processed cheese turns out 3,000,000 boxes a month.

Much of the footwear manufacture—like the jewellery—is still carried out as a cottage industry or by small family businesses, and when walking along a street in one of the small towns one often sees through an open doorway or window a solitary worker sitting at a machine. But there is now a move towards production in automated factories, which with admirable foresight have been concentrated in well-laid-out industrial estates on the outskirts of the two main towns, so that they do not spoil the beauty of the island. An outstanding example is the 'Industrial Polygon' outside Mahón, which includes a trades exhibition hall.

The shoe industry employs 50 per cent of the island's labour market. Ciudadela specialises in ladies' shoes. Their style and workmanship have a European reputation and are bought by Paris fashion houses. Mercadal specialises in men's sandals of soft cowhide with soles of tyre (rubber, guaranteed for 5,000 miles!). Alayor's craftsmen make men's shoes, and have supplied Prince Rainier of Monaco. Mahón makes slippers.

The manufacture of costume jewellery employs 20 per cent of the working population, and there are very large numbers of home workers as well as those in factories. The product is artistic in design and of excellent craftsmanship, and has its roots in the work of silversmiths in the nineteenth century.

These trades, shoe- and jewellery-making, suggest that Minorcans are clever with their hands, and this is borne out by a variety of other small industries. Among these are electrical accessories, calculating machines, leatherwork and toys. San Luis manufactures construction-kits for model ships, and one can visit the factory and see the final product in an exhibition room.

Another factory one can visit in Mahón makes gin, and the visitor is invited to taste a sample. It is also made at Ferrerias. It was a British introduction in the eighteenth century, and is said to be made to the original English recipe. A second industry which had British beginnings is furniture-making, based on a tradition of Chippendale and Hepplewhite. Modern Minorcan furniture can be of high quality and attractive design, and some of the original antique furniture can still be found in private houses like the Golden Farm at Mahón.

The first trickle of tourists did not arrive in Minorca until 1955. This late development was almost entirely due to the extremely poor external communications.

External communications

Some degree of inaccessibility may add to the charm of an island, but the desire to cut travelling time is not a new one. In the eighteenth century three weeks' sail from England via Gibraltar was considered tedious. When Britain was not at war with France, it was popular to travel by post-chaise from Calais via Paris, Lyons and Marseilles, and then by mail packet to Fornells in the north. If one did not run into a storm in the Gulf of Lyons, this could cut the journey to about fifteen days.

Two hundred years later, in 1949, it could take as long as five days. The only route was, as always, across France to Barcelona, then by the thrice-weekly steamer from there to Mahón. This boat service operated by the Compañia Trasmediterranea, has now been increased to daily sailings between July and September.

This service carried 61,138 passengers in 1965, and more than double that number—137,485—in 1972. It is now inadequate, and additional modern ships have recently been introduced. To meet this increase in traffic, enlargement of the commercial quay at Port Mahón is in progress, and a large modern passenger terminal is planned.

However, it was the advent of air travel that was decisive in making Minorca an important tourist centre. The first commercial flight from Barcelona to Mahón took place in 1949 in a DC3, operated by the newly formed Aviaco Company. This still operates a passenger and freight service, the flight taking about twenty minutes. It also flies between Palma (Majorca) and Mahón. The first charter flights from England to Minorca took place during the summer of 1955 in a Douglas DC3. They used the small airport at San Luis.

Six years later, in 1961, the total number of tourists was still only 1,500, although by 1964 it had risen to nearly 10,000. In the following year the figure rocketed to 113,853, of which 52,620 were air passengers, and by 1973 the total number of visitors exceeded half a million (there were 374,632 air passengers in 1972).

The new international airport which opened near San Clemente outside Mahón in 1969 largely contributed to this increase, but it is already too small for future requirements. For example, during one day in July 1973 seventy-four flights in and out were processed. The passenger reception centre and car parking facilities are being extended, and by 1976 the length of the runways will be increased to 2,750m to comply with the regulations for use by long-distance planes with heavy fuel loads. Automatic landing devices to international standards will also be installed.

Tourist developments

Minorcans have coped well with this influx, having undertaken a vast building programme to house the tourists, and established one more industry—building—which has brought still more prosperity, although it has drained more men from the land. There are at present about thirty-six hotels, excluding one-star hostelries. There is, however, more emphasis on villa developments—these are less likely to spoil the landscape—and there are more than thirty major ones, mostly around the more popular *playas*.

Strict government controls regulate the location and standard of building. Lessons learned from elsewhere in Spain are being heeded and 'concrete jungles' avoided. Additional capital from Madrid, Barcelona and Britain has poured in. Villas are mostly privately owned, mainly by the British, but also by Spanish, Dutch and other nationalities. Some owners sublet them through travel agencies to tourists as part of inclusive holidays by charter flights.

Two of the largest and most ambitious 'urbanisations' are at

'Shangri-la' (the developer's name) on the rolling downs over-looking the lake of Albufera, and Son Parc at the beach of Son Saura. Both of these are on the northern coast. At each, in addition to luxury villas, there will be golf courses, hotels, clubs, restaurants, swimming-pools and shops. In five to ten years' time these could be thriving new communities. The promoters, in selecting northern sites, have boldly decided to break the population pattern of countless centuries, and dared to confront the *tramontana*.

SOCIAL CONDITIONS

The increased wealth brought to the island has not radically changed Minorcans' way of life. Not all projects succeed, and much capital invested may not show returns for many years. But there is full employment and no poverty, and if the foreign resident hopes for domestic help, she will be fortunate to get it once a week at rates as high as she paid at home. With prosperity has come a measure of inflation, and prices of food are high. Wealth per capita in Spain is greatest in the Balearics, and the standard of living in Minorca is the third highest after Madrid and Barcelona.

The Minorcan housewife has a well-furnished house or flat, with modern sanitation, electricity, gas cooker and refrigerator. She is accustomed to buying frozen foods, and will shop in super-markets. Both she and her children will be well dressed, and her house will be scrupulously clean. If she lives in a village or the country, and is going out she will leave her key in the front door, in case a friend should call.

The public services at her disposal will be up-to-date, and for the most part adequate.

Electricity services

To meet the increasing requirements of mechanised farming and industry, and of tourism, bold steps were taken in 1973 to ensure more than adequate electrical power for the forseeable future.

Electricity for lighting purposes on a small scale was first introduced in Minorca by private enterprise early in the present century. GESA (Gas and Electrical Company), a nationalised firm based in Majorca, took over this responsibility in 1959, when it built the present oil-operated power station at the head of Port Mahón. At its inception this had a capacity for 3,000kW, which was increased to 17,000kW by 1973. As this was insufficient for future needs, GESA took the far-sighted step of bringing electrical power from Majorca by means of a submarine cable link, which will increase Minorca's electrical capacity sixfold to 100,000kW. The Mahón power-station will remain as an ancillary unit. This operation was carried out by an Italian firm with a world-wide reputation—Industria Pirelli—at a cost of £5½ million.

Four cables were laid from Cala Mesquida in Majorca (not to be confused with Minorca's beach of the same name) and Cala Bosch in the south-west corner of Minorca. Each cable was of record length—42km—had a diameter of 82mm, and weighed 750 tons. Before being laid, each cable was encased in an outer tube containing oil. In this sophisticated installation, provision is made for pumping oil into the submerged tubes. Three cables will be in constant use, and one held in reserve. The final stages of the installation were witnessed by top engineers from Britain, America and Canada, who were flown in for the occasion.

Water supply

Water is supplied by artesian wells, and is piped to towns, villages and tourist developments. Piped water supplied by municipal authorities is chlorinated and frequently tested, so that one may drink the tap-water. A modest water rate is paid.

Engineers are satisfied that water reserves are adequate for the forseeable future.

In country areas and in farmhouses generally, wells and *cisternas* (domestic reservoirs partly excavated underground) are the usual source of supply. These are common in Spain, and if their water level falls very low drinking water can be delivered.

Page 159 (above) Fiesta of Our Lady of Grace, Mahón, showing rampant horse and crowds. City Chambers in background; (below) the Yacht Club, Port Mahón

Page 160 Cala Galdana, the 'Queen of the Playas'

Postal services

Town post offices conform to modern standards; village ones are more primitive. The latter are often also small bars and sell cigarettes. One must not commit the social blunder of licking a stamp, a moist pad being provided. As is general on the European continent stamps are also sold at tobacconists. Telegrams are delivered the day after receipt by the post office. Philatelists will find the wide variety of Spanish pictorial stamps of high artistic quality, often illustrating their history and art.

Telephones

The island has an automatic-dialling telephone system, and this system has recently been extended to most of the large cities in peninsular Spain. Domestic telephones are common in the towns, and the island has more than 6,000 subscribers, but they have not reached individual homes in the tourist settlements. Visitors wishing to make a trunk call overseas may do so either from their hotel, from the airport, or by going to the Central Telephone Exchange at Mahón or Ciudadela. These are small, but efficient, and the telephonists are extremely helpful. The procedure is not difficult.

Transport

Mahón had a bus service as early as 1911. Today, public transport is served by a network of modern motor coaches, which connect Mahón and Ciudadela, together with all the main centres of population. There are regular services between the airport and Mahón. The tourist town of Cala'n Porter also has a year-round service to Mahón. Taxis are available at fixed rates depending on destination (they do not have meters). Even if the visitor is not presented with a written tariff, he need not fear overcharging, as Minorcans are honest. It is advisable to hire a car when on holiday and this can be done at the airport if desired. The Seat 600, the Spanish version of the Fiat, is the

K   161 car commonly used—it is as sturdy as a mule on rough country roads.

It is not known exactly when the first car reached Minorca. The earliest recorded horseless carriage was driven by coal and was very noisy, sounding like some form of steam-engine. The first cars were owned by a few of the wealthier farmers just before World War I, and became commoner after 1918. The commonest car in the early twenties was the Ford Model T. Other early cars seen at rallies are a 1922 Renault, a 1925 Oldsmobile and a 1931 Adler. Right up to about 1968 British and other cars more than twenty-five years old were a common sight on Minorcan roads; the construction of spare parts presented no problem to ingenious local engineers and blacksmiths. Nowadays the Seats, the Renaults and the Simcas have replaced them.

Apart from the congestion in Mahón and Ciudadela road traffic is pleasantly light, and the foreign motorist is helped on his way by a profusion of international road-signs and yellow lines.

Mahón's progressive mayor and counsellors plan to close much of the centre of the town to motor traffic, and construct a ring road round it to Villa Carlos.

FUTURE TRENDS

Minorcans show no signs of losing their heads as a result of the avalanche of tourists that has overtaken them. As a single example, they have opened a School of Tourism in Mahón to study and guide them in all its implications. Looking to the future, Mahón municipality in 1973 held a public exhibition on their 'Plan 1975' in which they gave details of ambitious projects for the city, and invited criticism and suggestions. Social improvements included an increase in educational and hospital services, and provision of up-to-date facilities for handicapped children and for the elderly.

More spectacular were their recreational plans. The new Freginal Park near the centre of the city, measuring 18,000 square metres, will be made possible by the use of ecclesiastical land. It will have underground parking accommodation for 600 cars, and in addition to a children's play area (a feature of all parks in Minorca), there will be a sports section, gardens, a miniature zoo, shops and restaurant, and an open-air stage. The inner part of Port Mahón is to be developed as an aquatic sports centre, to achieve which the municipality has acquired the historic Isla del Rey ('The King's Island') as its main base. A new pedestrian way will lead from the city centre at Plaza Miranda down the cliffs to the quay, with rock gardens, steps, floodlighting and vantage-points over the port.

Minorcans may be becoming more sophisticated, and internationally minded, but are in no danger of losing their identity, for nothing can take away their individuality as islanders. They have taken active steps to redress any opposite tendencies in their young people, by fostering a new interest in their history and heritage. The results can best be seen by examining further their island life and culture.

10   ISLAND LIFE AND CULTURE

MINORCANS have a deep interest in cultural pursuits, for which they have a long tradition. Their contacts with the British in the eighteenth century widened the mental horizons of the educated, and Mahón's first cultural society was founded during the second British occupation in 1778. Its members were mostly Minorcan lawyers and intellectuals, who carried out an ambitious programme of debates, literary readings and translation of foreign works into the Minorquin language. The society suffered a decline during the subsequent Spanish occupation, but flourished again in the early nineteenth century, when it led a revival in Catalan literature.

Today the Minorcan's studious and inquiring mind is still applied to history, art, music and literature. When the winter *tramontana* blows, it is refreshing to find a people who make and organise their own cultural activities, and do not slavishly follow the small screen.

Out of Spain's estimated budget for 1974, 18 per cent (£73 million or $220 million) was allocated to 'education and culture'. The figure is substantial, but the linking of education with culture is notable. In Minorca they do in fact go hand in hand. In addition to its schools and colleges, Mahón has two remarkable cultural societies, founded in the early part of the present century, which continue to be strongly influential. The first is the *Ateneo* (Athenaeum), and the second the *Casa de Cultura*. In 1973 a third society, the International Centre for Culture and the Arts, opened its doors, under American inspiration and leadership.

164

The Ateneo

The Ateneo is a scientific, literary and arts association founded in 1905, and is the most important cultural centre on the island. Its modest and old fashioned rooms in the street called Conde de Cifentes (behind the Explanada) quite belie its industry and influence. In addition to a library of over 10,000 volumes, and a reading room with some 100 foreign magazines and journals, it publishes annually its own historical and scientific review, the *Revista de Menorca*, which first appeared in 1888. The scope of subjects dealt with is wide, but the most important have been history and archaeology. In this respect a great service to knowledge has been performed, making possible the publication of much original research.

The association also sponsors and holds art and photographic exhibitions, runs courses on the arts, and offers substantial prizes annually in a wide range of fields. In recent years these have included poetry, the novel, journalism, music, social and natural sciences, archaeology, sociology, tourism, architecture, films and history. Such a body is unusual in a town of only 25,000 inhabitants.

The Ateneo also has a large natural-history collection of over 17,000 marine specimens, and a notable map collection. Re-issues of some of the more popular reviews are beginning to appear in local bookshops.

La Casa de Cultura

The Casa de Cultura does not represent a state cultural body as its name might suggest, but is a library and museum in a dignified neo-classical eighteenth-century house (formerly known as the Casa Mercadal) in the Plaza de la Conquista. It was bought and given to the city of Mahón by a citizen interested in the arts—Don José Codina Villalonga—and converted to its present use. In addition to the facilities mentioned, it has an auditorium for lectures. Its modern library houses over 20,000 volumes, and hundreds of periodicals. The visitor will be impressed by its scope and atmosphere of scholarship; by its silence and small groups of senior school pupils studying at tables, the whole scene reminding one of a university town. The reader will recollect that the Casa was built on the former site of the castle of Mahón, and he should not miss the precipitous view down to the port from one of the library windows.

The museum is well worth a visit, and contains many relics from Phoenician and Roman times, as well as part of the mausoleum of Sir Richard Kane from the former St Philip's Castle, which had been destroyed by the French in 1784. In an anteroom to the museum is a loan collection from Mr Jim Maps illustrating the three British occupations of the island in the eighteenth century. Some fine engravings of St Philip's Fort are particularly interesting. The museum houses many local historical archives, maps and engravings.

International Centre for Culture

The International Centre for Culture and the Arts opened in Mahón in October 1973, and as its name implies it hopes to spread its influence beyond the island. Its doors are old ones, for it occupies a formerly derelict building, adjoining the church of San Francisco, which was once a fifteenth-century monastery and later a nunnery. Its founder and first director is Mrs Alicia Neath, an American of South American and Spanish descent, and a noted sculptress. She is assisted by her daughter, and a Minorcan, Señor Francisco Pons Montenari.

The prospectus offers a wide choice of classes: sculpture, painting, ceramics, pottery, photography, music, art, drama, ballet and physical culture and languages. It is open to all races and ages, and tuition is in both Spanish and English, by professional teachers. It is hoped to run special courses during the summer months to attract visiting students.

The director was able to enlist American official interest in the project in addition to local co-operation. The Spanish government placed the building at the disposal of the Centre.

Mahón municipality contributes to the cost of the project. The American Navy has also provided substantial help, thus forming a new link between America and Minorca.

Cultural 'Week of the Month'

As well as this more academic side of cultural life, Mahón municipality organises throughout the year a 'week of the month', each week being devoted to one aspect of the life of the people. A full programme of events is published in advance, and these are entered into by the Mahónese with as much enthusiasm as they devote to their fiestas. There are competitions between groups and prizes offered, often by local business firms. In some ways they resemble British musical and other festivals.

The following list of 'weeks' from January to December give some idea of their variety: Balearic Theatre, Sport, Opera, Country Life, Children's Week, Nautical Week, Civics, Trade (Jewellery), Film Week, Christmas. It is not possible to deal with each in detail, but the very active local theatre, music and opera groups in Mahón are particularly worth mentioning. The 'Children's Week' is singled out by way of illustration. It takes place when the school year has finished, at the end of June. Like all Spaniards, Minorcans adore their children, but surely nowhere else could end-of-term celebrations last for a week, and require such stamina.

In 1973 the programme was as follows:

Saturday evening. Official opening of exhibition of school handiwork in the Town Hall. Competitions and open-air acting performance in the Esplanade. Grand bonfire with burning of effigies, ending with a 'powerful and very loud firework'.

Sunday evening. Open-air party in the Esplanade—given by the local ice-cream factory. Conjuror and illusionist followed.

Monday evening. Modelmaking competition with prizes, followed by children's Fair, music and games.

Tuesday evening. Play in local theatre in Minorquin language.

Wednesday morning. End-of-term picnic to Es Grau beach for sand-castle contest, financed by local estate developer.

167

Evening: musical festival by the School of Music and pupils under leading local conductor in the Opera House.

Thursday. End-of-year speeches and prize-giving in local theatre. Party with sideshows in new industrial complex given by leading firm. A sudden serious note—Round Table Discussion between fathers and senior pupils on teen-age problems of life and education.

Friday. Sailing regatta in Port Mahón. Speed-boat racing (pupils taken as passengers). Dance group. Municipal band. Final firework display.

Saturday. Exhibitions of pupils' best paintings and drawings.

At the end of this marathon, these fortunate children enter on three months' summer holidays during which they enjoy the beaches as much as do the tourists.

NEWSPAPERS

Minorca has one daily newspaper, called *Menorca*, published in Mahón, and one weekly newspaper, *El Iris*, published in Ciudadela. In the past, *Menorca* has issued an occasional supplement in English to assist tourists on their holidays, and during the summer months of 1973 a monthly English newspaper called *Roqueta* appeared to meet a similar need. Foreign newspapers—British, German and American—are available, usually on the day after issue.

By far the most important newspaper on the island is *Menorca*, which is an institution. It has passed its 9,000th issue, and is in its thirty-fourth year of publication, the first copy appearing in 1941. Its first two or three pages are devoted to international and Spanish news, and a similar number at the end to sports—mainly football. The central section is headed 'Minorca and the Minorcans—Each and All' and is a daily chronicle of life on the island, which it faithfully and fairly reflects. It maintains an extremely high standard of journalism, with frequent articles of an informative nature on local topics, interviews with local personalities, both humble and famous, even poems. Its coverage of the town's cultural activities is objective and full, and there is a welcome absence of syndicated material.

LITERATURE

A distinction has to be made between literature in Castilian Spanish, and in the Minorquin (Catalan) dialect. The former obviously reaches a wider public. Written or literary Minorquin differs quite considerably in idiom and vocabulary from the spoken language, so that although Minorquin is still the common spoken tongue of Minorcans among themselves, many are unable to write it correctly. As in other countries with an ancient surviving language a small group of local writers and poets have done much in recent years to keep literary Minorquin alive.

The most notable modern Minorcan writer was D. Angel Ruiz Pablo (1865–1927). He was born in Villa Carlos and wrote both prose and verse in Castilian as well as Minorquin. In recent years some of his narrative prose has been adapted for the theatre. Another writer, D. Francisco Camps Mercadal, has written a book on island folklore, *Folklore Menorqui de la pagesia*.

Among Minorcan writers in Castilian Spanish, special mention is made of Mario Verdaguer's *Piedras y Viento* ('Stones and Wind'), a delightful novel about Minorca in the eighteenth century during the British occupation. It is not yet available in English.

The majority of Minorcan writers have chosen historical or archaeological themes. Over a thousand papers have been written on the island's megalithic monuments, a large number of them by Minorcans. The chief of these is a comprehensive reference book entitled *Prehistoria de las Baleares*, by J. Mascaró Pasarius, which is well illustrated. Only two others deserve mention. Minorca's greatest historian was Francisco Hernández Sanz, who published a comprehensive history of the island in Spanish entitled *Compendio de Geografía y Historia de Menorca* in

1908. He is still greatly honoured in Mahón, where cultural prizes are often named after him. The second is the only biography in existence on Sir Richard Kane, the *Gobierno de Sir Richard Kane en Menorca*, a slim volume by A. Victory, published in 1924.

MUSIC AND ART

Minorcans are musical and have a number of musical societies. They are interested in both classical and modern works. Mahón's 'opera week' has been mentioned; and an International Festival of Song was held in 1973 at which singers from seven European countries competed. All Minorcan towns have their town bands, and Mahón sometimes invites guest bands and orchestras with a wide reputation to her more important fiestas. Minorcan has a handsome Opera House with over eighty boxes, built in 1824 by an Italian architect.

The organ of Santa Maria

But the musical pride of Mahón is its monumental pipe organ in the church of Santa Maria, designed by the Swiss organ-builder Kyburz and completed by him in 1810. It has four keyboards, fifty-seven organ stops and 3,006 sound pipes; clearly not for the amateur.

It is an organ whose history goes back to the Napoleonic Wars. In 1810, although Minorca had been returned to Spain by Britain eight years earlier, the British Mediterranean fleet under Admiral Collingwood was still protecting the island against invasion by French forces, and Collingwood was staying briefly at *El Fonduco* in Port Mahón. Minorcans asked him to arrange a 'safe conduct' for the great pipe organ to be brought by sea from Barcelona, and to help negotiate a similar agreement with the French. This was the last of Collingwood's many services to Minorca. He was a sick and lonely man, who had not been able to visit his wife and daughters in England for over five years. He sailed from Port Mahón shortly afterwards for home, but died at sea the day after leaving port. There was no requiem for the admiral.

The organ's second adventure was during the Spanish Civil War of 1936–9. It narrowly escaped destruction by Nationalist rebels, and was only saved by the bodily intervention of the aged writer Hernández Sanz, who suggested they might care to spare it for their secular celebrations after victory.

The organ has had many gifted organists, and recently underwent a substantial renovation.

Folk music and dance

There is a lively interest in the island in the preservation of folk songs in the Minorquin dialect, fostered by several folk groups. The oldest of these songs are associated with dances, and are believed to have been introduced by the soldiers of Alphonso III of Aragon after the conquest of 1287, later becoming modified and altered to suit the changing life and attitudes of the people. Some of the old songs had a religious theme and these are still popular, such as '*El Bon Jesuset*' ('The Good Child Jesus') and '*Un Senor Damunt d'un Roc*' ('A Master Mounted on an Ass').

Señor Mercadal, a leading musician and conductor in Mahón, has recently composed and recorded many popular folk songs, mostly based on Minorcan legends which have survived orally from Moorish times. The most popular are '*Su Novia Aljandar*' ('The Bride of Algendar'); a Minorcan serenade called '*Surt a Sa Fenestra*' ('Come to thy Window'), and the gayer '*Si em Casare*' ('If I were to marry').

The dances have a smoother and more soothing tempo than that associated with Spanish music, in spite of the customary castanets accompanying the guitars, and the woman's movements are more restricted than the man's. The commonest local dances are a form of the fandango, and the Minorcan *jota*—a speciality of the town of Mercadal. On a formal occasion for tourists traditional Minorcan costume will be worn.

Special mention must be made of a Scottish dance which the

people of Villa Carlos adopted from Highland troops and their families in the eighteenth century, and which they still dance at their fiestas. It is called the '*Ball d'Escocia*' ('The Ball of Scotland'), and its twelve dancers wear a kind of tartan and carry little sticks. It is accompanied by a solitary fife with drums, and sounds like the plaintive song of a Highland exile.

Art

Because of the brilliant quality of its light, Minorca attracts artists, and some Minorcans are accomplished painters. Rural scenes, showing shadows cast by the sloping roofs of farmhouses, or a lonely cove, are common and satisfying subjects. Attractive water-colours can be bought as reminders of one's holiday.

Minorca has had several famous visiting painters and one of its own. The Italian painter Guiseppe Chiesa settled and married in Minorca in the eighteenth century, and opened an art academy in Mahón. He sent his pupil, a Minorcan called Pascual Calbo Caldes, to Italy to study art. The latter was a brilliant artist, who specialised in portraiture but liked to paint peasant children. He became court-painter to the Empress Maria Theresa at the age of twenty-seven, and later returned to Minorca after a brilliant career.

As we have already read, Sir Joshua Reynolds visited Minorca in 1749, on his way to Italy, and is reputed to have painted a number of portraits of officers of the garrison.

FIESTAS

No account of the island's cultural life is complete without a description of her fiestas, in which Minorcans participate with great enthusiasm.

The word 'fiesta' is nowadays applied to any holiday—national or saint's day—and all are celebrated with equal gaiety when any early religious devotions have been completed. Since each town and village has its own patron saint, the summer months seem a succession of such holidays. The first intimation the innocent visitor receives on approaching his nearest small town may be closed shops and 'no entry' signs completely blocking off its main street, which is completely given over to the celebrations—even to equestrian contests. At night he will be disturbed by fireworks and song, and on the following day restaurants and bars will close to allow staff to recover.

Minorca's main fiestas are unique in that they re-enact some outstanding event in the island's history, or portray a period, as in an historical pageant. In spite of their gaiety, Minorcans feel that they are taking part in an act of commemoration. The best example of this is the Fiesta of St John at Ciudadela, which takes place each year on 24 and 25 June. It has been listed by the Spanish government as being of 'international tourist interest', and merits a short description.

Fiesta of San Juan

The festival of St John commemorates San Juan, the patron saint of Ciudadela. Essentially it is a procession or cavalcade on horseback, which halts at intervals on its route to indulge in various performances and rites. The horsemen are made up of representatives from the traditional medieval classes: nobility, clergy, peasants and craftsmen. The patron of the fiesta is known as the 'Caixer Senyor', and together with the other riders is appointed each year.

The traditional dress of the riders varies with their rank, but from its nature cannot be as old as the rites performed. In general it consists of spurred riding boots, breeches, tailed coat, two-pointed hat and sword. Craftsmen can be recognised by their black suits, and peasants by their white trousers. The patron seems to be in evening dress, except for his white riding breeches and long boots. He wears white gloves.

The procession and its rituals and trappings have a medieval air, and the festival is believed to have originated in the early fourteenth century. Both the colourful trappings of the horses and flag carried by the standard-bearer display a white

173

Maltese cross on a red background, which was the insignia of both the Knights of St John of Jerusalem and Knights of Malta. It is thought that some of the latter may have taken part in the Christian conquest of Minorca in 1287 by Alphonso III of Aragon, an inference that is in keeping with the equestrian feats of the fiesta which resemble medieval jousts and tournaments. Leading this splendid cavalcade of horsemen, to the music of flageolet and drum, rides a humble herald mounted on a donkey.

On the Sunday before 24 June, the festival is opened by a short ceremony in which a young man, possibly representing St John, clad in lambskin and decked with flowers, carries a live lamb through the town, accompanied by a small group. The main celebrations begin on 24 June, and start with a parade round the Borne Square, after which the cavalcade goes on a 'pilgrimage' to the Hermitage of St John, 5km outside Ciudadela. On its return it stops at Es Pla, on open space at the head of the port, where traditional games on horseback and mock jousts are carried out. The characteristic rearing of the horses on their hindlegs throughout the whole festival is supposed to imitate these jousts. A pre-arranged circuit of the old city is then carried out, and the people are out in their thousands, cheering and throwing nuts at horsemen and each other. In their excitement some vie with each other to invite horse and rider into the vestibule or patio of their house as this is considered to bring good fortune; this is not as foolhardy as it sounds, as they have taken the precaution of barricading their inner rooms.

The final part of the procession is through the narrow shopping street of José Maria Quadrado, opening out into the spacious Borne Square. This is the climax, and the signal for unrestrained gaiety. The crowds mix with the rearing horses, and jollity continues far into the night, ending with a firework display.

Fiesta of Our Lady of Grace

Each of the other towns and villages celebrates its saint's day with equestrian displays, such as the fiesta of San Lorenzo at Alayor, and of St Bartholomew at Ferrerias, both in August.

Only Mahón's fiesta in the first week of September in honour of 'the Virgin, Our Lady of Grace', is in sharp contrast. Looking forward and not back, it has become a Civic or Festival Week in the modern sense, and a whole week of gay celebrations precedes its single day of religious ceremonies. For the celebrations of the fiesta in 1973, the mayor's committee drew up a programme of events from which no possible recreation or spectacle was omitted, and the organisation and showmanship were superb.

Events started with a civic reception to representatives from the sister-city of Barcelona, and the crowning of the Barcelona mayor's daughter as 'Floral Queen of the Fiesta'. Prizes were given for floral displays, and the prize poem of welcome was read by the Catalan Poet Laureate. This was followed by an 'Exhibition 1975', displaying the ambitious projects already outlined, and the opening of a three-day international Festival of Song in the Opera House.

The second day (Sunday) offered shooting and cycling contests, a football match between Ibiza and Mahón, with 'majorettes' in red-and-white uniforms to parade and entertain the crowds. For the children there was a mammoth party on the Esplanade, financed by a local firm.

During the week, interspersed with the Song Festival and opera, were kart-racing, free aeroplane flights, excursions to the King's Island, and sailing regattas in Port Mahón. An aircraft of the Iberia Line was christened *City of Mahón* by the mayoress, and Friday brought a Parade of Giants and Battle of Flowers, with brass bands. On Saturday there were mass parachute-drops by the Spanish air force.

On the closing day of the Festival a solemn procession to the church of Santa Maria took place, in which an image of the

175

Virgin Mary was borne aloft. All the civic and public bodies were represented, and local bands were joined by those from the American and Italian navies.

Christmas in Minorca

Minorcans have an exuberance and flair for showmanship in their fiestas, and this is particularly noticeable in those which their children share, as at Christmas. As in other countries, shops are decorated and full of exotic toys, the streets illuminated and made gay with Christmas trees and cribs of the Nativity. Bands play in the squares. The giving of presents, however, does not take place until Twelfth Night (6 January), and is associated with *Los Reyes Magos* (the Three Kings or Wise Men), who brought gifts to the Infant Jesus. This is made the occasion for a jollification for the children of Mahón, in which press, army and navy all take a part.

On the previous day the local newspaper publishes the following mock telegram from the Three Kings:

Office of Origin: The East
Destination: Mahón. *Addressees:* Children of the city. Supercargo of toys arriving at Commercial dock today at 6.30 pm Stop.
Senders' Names: Gaspar, Melchior and Baltazar.

The children assembled on the quay, having been told that the ship arriving from the East is an 'atomic' one too large to enter the port, welcome the Three Kings (suitably attired), who are brought ashore by a naval launch, and received by the deputy governor of the island, by the military governor and by the mayor. After welcoming speeches the Three Kings go in procession through the city in decorated 'state' coaches, preceded by pages bearing symbolic gifts for the child Jesus.

In 1973, a new event was, however, reported in the local press two weeks earlier—the arrival of 'papa Noel' (Father Christmas) by air at Mahón Aero Club, with toys for the children of the sponsoring school, and a freight of toffees for all comers.

11 PLACES TO VISIT—THINGS TO DO

MANY holidaymakers visiting Minorca stay for as little as two weeks. This is unfortunate for there is so much to see, and gives barely time to relax and get the feeling of the island. Three weeks or a month would be better. The following notes will help the short-term visitor to use his time to best advantage.

The first essential is a good island map, and these are on sale at most tourist centres and hotels at small cost. Those recommended are the *Mapa Turistica de Menorca* by J. Mascaró Pasarius which has a plan of Mahón on the back, and the larger *Mapa Arqueologica de Menorca* by the same author. In addition to modern details shown in the former map, this shows the main megalithic sites and villages, and has plans of Mahón, Ciudadela, Alayor and Mercadal on the reverse. Another good map is published by the Firestone tyre firm, which shows the island's contours, and has a great deal of other information, with plans and street indexes of Mahón and Ciudadela. On none of these is the grading of roads up-to-date, and some of the new roads will not be shown. Maps of the standard of the British Ordnance Survey have to be specially ordered.

THE TWENTY-FOUR BEST BEACHES

As much depends on individual tastes, it is only possible to classify these by types and location. The following are all situated on the south coast, and developed in varying degree as tourist centres with villas to rent and/or hotel accommodation:

L   177

The first two are very large and can together accommodate thousands of sun-seekers. Cala'n Porter and Galdana are particularly safe for young children, as the beach slopes very gradually to the water's edge. Beaches on the south coast as yet undeveloped but the most recommended are:

Cala Turqueta	Son Saura
Macarella	Macarelleta
Mitjana	Trebaluger
Es Canutells	Binidali

Of these Cala Turqueta is outstanding. It is approached by a reasonably good country road from Ciudadela (the route is best followed on the tourist map). With pine trees to its water's edge, and the clearest of blue seas, it is a delightful spot. In high season there may be no more than a dozen people there, and off season one will probably be alone. The same applies to the twin beaches of Macarella and Macarelleta, and to Mitjana. These three are best approached on foot through the pine-woods on either side of Galdana—a pleasant and easy walk, with many Mediterranean flowers, and in late autumn purple heather, bordering one's path.

For the pioneer, a stiff climb over many walls and a rocky hillside takes one to Trebaluger. It is as yet more easily reached by sea. Es Canutells and Binidali are small fishing inlets of charm.

On the north coast are the following beaches, all under tourist development:

Arenal d'en Castell	Binimel-La
Cala Tirant	Es Grau
Cala Morell	Cala Mesquida
Son Parc (Son Saura)	

There are several other large beaches on the north coast, which are at present undeveloped, the most notable being Algaiarens.

On the west coast near Ciudadela are Cala Blanca and Cala Santandria, which have hotels, but are rather small and inclined to be crowded in summer.

Where to be alone

There are many small beaches, especially in the north, where one can be alone. Here one is in a dilemma: to tell or not to tell? They are often close to the major beaches, and it is exciting to discover them for oneself. The map often gives one a clue. Binimel-La, Es Grau and Castell all have minor coves nearby, and there are some on the route to the Favaritx and Cavalleria lighthouses. Near the last is a small beach near the old Roman port of Sanitja. In general it is best to avoid going at weekends when other people may have the same idea.

There are two delightful tiny beaches on the islet of Colom, off Es Grau. A local boatman will take one by motor-boat to the island and leave one there for a day. He has a good memory and one is in no danger of being marooned. On the way out he asks which of the two beaches—*sol o sombra* (sun or shade)—one prefers. The shady one is recommended in summer: an arc of silver sand, crystal clear blue sea, and tamarisk trees to the water's edge. The tiny friendly lizards peculiar to Isla Colom shyly scamper over one's picnic box.

SCENIC DRIVES

If time is limited, a drive from Mahón to Ciudadela should include a stop at the small inland town of Mercadal, to drive to the top of Monte Toro. The road is easy, and the view panoramic, especially towards Fornells in the north. After passing the town of Ferrerias a visit should be made to the Naveta des Tudons (boat-grave) sign-posted on the left a few kilometres out of Ciudadela.

Probably the most scenic drive on the island is to the Cavalleria lighthouse in the north (take the sign-posted road towards Binimel-Là at Mercadal and follow the map). The road passes a medieval fortified farmhouse and later the old Roman port of Sanitja. The view southward over the island from the precincts of the lighthouse, the panorama of sea, cliffs and hills in the background is outstanding.

Some of the best scenic drives should include walks. Those from Galdana through the pinewoods to Mitjana or Macarella have few equals, and excursions along the shores of Albufera lake or Port Addaya are equally rewarding.

MEGALITHIC SETTLEMENTS

Even the visitor who may not be particularly interested in these should visit a few, if only to appreciate the island's atmosphere. The sites usually command fine views, and make ideal picnic spots.

With a car the four most important taulas can be seen in a morning. These are:

Trepucó   Talatí de Dalt
Torralba d'en Salort   Torelló

Trepucó is the largest and one of the oldest taulas, and lies on the outskirts of Mahón, a few hundred yards beyond the end of the street called Cos de Gracia. Its main talayot is unusual in being partly encircled by an eighteenth-century gun emplacement, from which the Duc de Crillon once tried to terrorise the inhabitants of Mahón. When a Cambridge University team excavated the site in 1932, all but the top seven feet of the giant taula were buried in undergrowth and rubble, and it was a favourite vantage-point of small boys. Dr Margaret Murray, the team's leader (an experienced archaeologist who subsequently wrote about it in her autobiography *My First Hundred Years*), found the remains of eleven other talayots on the site, and very early (pre-Bronze Age) hand-worked pottery.

Taking the road to San Clemente, one can turn off right on

a country lane to Torelló, where an opportunity can be taken to see the mosaic floor of its ancient Byzantine basilica. Returning to the main road and proceeding to Alayor via the Cala'n Porter road, stop at Torralba d'en Salort, where in addition to a large talayot is a particularly good example of a taula whose *circulo* has recently been excavated. There is also a fine hypostyle court. A few yards away is the ancient well of Na Patarrá, probably dating to 800 BC. Returning to Mahón via Alayor, Talatí de Dalt can be visited. This is also a major prehistoric site with much of interest. Less known are the huddled dwellings of the prehistoric village of Alcaidus nearby.

Other outstanding megalithic sites dating from the Bronze Age are Torre d'en Gaumés (Alayor District) and the walled town of Son Catlar, near Ciudadela. Torre d'en Gaumés is a very large ancient town on a hill, with three talayots, a broken taula with sanctuary, and hypostyle courts, caves, numerous ancient streets, and circular mounds of stones which were former dwellings.

There are over one thousand megalithic buildings in Minorca, so that it is not practical to give a list. The best list in English is to be found in F. Chamberlin's book, *Balearics and their Peoples* (John Lane, 1927). This is now out of print, but still obtainable from libraries.

SPORTS

Facilities for all kinds of sport are available in Minorca, especially for those connected with the sea.

Sailing. At the time of writing, sailing dinghys may be hired at Port Mahón, Son Bou, Galdana and Castell beaches, and tuition is available at Port Mahón and Son Bou. For the enthusiast, more sophisticated facilities are available at the Club Maritimo in Mahón, where there is a summer programme of regattas. There is a Balearic Snipe Class Championship in July, and a national trophy in the same class is also competed for annually with entries from all over Spain.

In addition to the Snipe and Optimist, a new class has recently been introduced—the '470' dinghy. This a moulded-plastic craft, with built-in buoyancy, and is 4·7m in length. It has been adopted for the 1976 Olympics. There are Nautical Clubs at Ciudadela and Fornells.

Subaqua Sports. Tuition and advice on this is available at Port Mahón and at Cala'n Porter. It is possible to explore submerged ancient settlement sites and wrecks. This is an exciting sport in Minorca for the skilled. The remains of Greek amphorae and pottery have been found.

Water-skiing is available at almost all the beaches which cater for tourists.

Swimming. Minorca is renowned for its safe and delightful swimming, but beaches frequented by tourists use a flag-warning system when storms are imminent. Such conditions rarely occur during the summer months. Most of the hotels have swimming-pools.

Golf. Three golf courses are at present under construction, located at Binixeca, at 'Shangri-la' and at Son Parc.

Tennis is also available to visitors in many parts of the island.

Watching Sports. Mahón and Ciudadela each have a football stadium and a hippodrome (racecourse). At the latter, trotting cart races are also a feature.

BIRD-WATCHING

To northern European visitors accustomed to seeing thousands of sea-birds on cliffs and offshore islands, Minorcan coasts seem silent and bare. The herring gull and cormorant nest on its cliffs, but in small numbers. The Lake of Albufera, however, teems with mallard, teal and partridge, while grey and purple heron and numerous waders frequent its shallows, and an occasional exotic pink flamingo displays its red and black wings as it takes off.

Minorca has long been a protected island for birds, as a staging-post on summer and winter migrations. Albufera is in particular a bird sanctuary, but the effects of tourist development on its bird ecology have recently caused local naturalists concern, and further protective measures are in hand. Other good sites for bird observation are at Fornells and Port Addaya. Inland the peregrine falcon and other predatory birds are often seen hovering overhead, as well as an occasional golden eagle, with characteristic splayed and upturned wing-tips. There are numerous smaller birds—swallows, warblers and thrushes, not forgetting the friendly robin.

About 180 separate species are said to have been identified in Minorca, but previous lists deal with the Balearics as a whole. No separate list of the birds of Minorca has previously been compiled in English, and for this reason the sightings in 1974 given in Appendix C are both important and likely to bring new recruits to an absorbing hobby.

FOOD

Food often plays an important part in one's holiday. Minorca is not a gourmet's paradise, and what one is offered depends a good deal on where one is staying. As elsewhere in Europe, hotels tend to offer 'international' menus, and their quality and variety are usually in proportion to the price. Minorca has many excellent hotels and restaurants both in town and country, so that it would be invidious to mention some and not others.

Minorca has few regional dishes of distinction. The traditional local dishes are often soups. It has been said that these are historically a 'heritage of the hungry' and have their origin in meagre times when food was scarce. The two most common are *zarzuela* soup which has a basis of fish, and *gazpacho*, a vegetable soup which is taken cold. Fish is not as plentiful as one would expect in an island, for the tideless Mediterranean is lacking in plankton, the basic food of larval fishes. Restaurants, especially at Villa Carlos and at Fornells, however, specialise in sea-food. In addition to shell-fish, lobsters and *calamares* (squids), the most palatable are red mullet (*salmonete*), sole (*lenguado*), *denton* (there is no English for this name), tunny—first introduced by the Romans—and a large species of sardine. *Paella* is a popular dish, and is made of saffron rice cooked with sea-food, oil and peppers and often including octopus. Salads and Spanish omelettes are common entrées, and one must not forget the famous mayonnaise sauce which is served with meat as well as salads.

A word on drinks must be added. These are cheap on the island. Gin is manufactured locally and Minorcans drink it with a slice of lemon and soda water (they call it *pallofa*), or else neat. Sangría is a refreshing drink to take with lunch in the hot weather. It consists of red wine served in large jugs in which float sliced fresh fruits—apples, oranges and peaches. If desired it can be laced with brandy, liqueurs and cinnamon. Spanish champagne and brandies are also popular. One rarely sees an intoxicated Minorcan, perhaps because they drink wines from an early age.

Both in and out of season, Minorca has a number of night-clubs for tourists. These are mainly located at Villa Carlos, Mahón and San Luis.

THE SIESTA

One of the best things to learn to do in Minorca is to adopt the Spanish custom of taking an afternoon siesta. This is the reason why Mahón and Ciudadela are completely deserted from two till nearly five and are lively in the evenings and at night. If one rises reasonably early in the mornings, this is not a slothful habit, and also keeps the older among us refreshed and relaxed. Like the Minorcans one can then stay up longer at night, thus getting almost two days for one.

With this mathematical thought, we conclude our account of the Summer Island.

INFORMATION FOR VISITORS

How to reach Minorca

ONE may fly direct from London to Minorca by Iberia Airlines, the journey taking just under two hours.

As an alternative a travel agent can usually arrange a charter flight inclusive of hotel or villa to most of the main tourist spots already described, and this will be cheaper than independent travel. If interested, one should contact firms specialising in these, such as Marshall Sutton Ltd, 7–9 Butcher Row, Beverly, Yorkshire, or Owners' Services Ltd, Broxbourne House, Broxbourne, who will arrange for you to be met on arrival. Special charter flights are also run at Easter and Christmas.

Alternative ways of reaching Minorca from England are by car across France to Barcelona, and then by night steamer from there to Mahón. A more leisurely route is by Swedish Lloyd Car Ferry from Southampton to Bilbao in northern Spain (thirty-six hours), and then drive (with one night stop) the 400 miles to Barcelona. The cheapest way from London is by luxury coach from Victoria Station to Barcelona (thirty-six hours). This can be arranged through Consort Travel, 9 Warwick Street, London, W1.

From the United States one may either fly to London and use any of these methods, or fly to Madrid, and from there to Mahón the whole journey taking about eight to nine hours.

Hotels

Your travel agent will guide you. There are at present only three four-star hotels. These are Port Mahón Hotel (Mahón),

Hotel Audax at Galdana beach, and Santo Tomas Hotel at the beach of the same name. There are over a dozen three-star hotels at the main tourist *playas*.

When to go

The season runs from early May until the end of October. July and August are the busiest and hottest months, and there is much to be said for an early or late holiday. October, and even November, are delightful, and costs will be lower.

Car hire

There are numerous self-drive hire firms on the island. A car can be hired at the airport. In August it is advisable to book through your travel agent in advance. An international driving licence is advisable.

Currency

The peseta is the unit. Money may be carried by travellers' cheques, or use made of one's Bank Card, under the Euro-cheque system, which operates at most local banks. American Express Cards are also used.

Local travel agencies

There are a number of these in Mahón and Ciudadela. Mahón has a branch of Cooks, in Calvo Sotelo Street. These agencies can arrange local excursions by sea; this is an interesting way of exploring the coast line.

Consulates

The nearest British and American consulates are at Palma, Majorca. Their addresses are Avenida Jaime 3, Nos 23 and 67, respectively. Mahón has, however, French, Italian, Dutch and Greek consulates. If one is in any difficulty over passports or cars, Minorcans do not deal with government departments direct, but go to a *Gestoria*, who is an agent who will fill up your forms and deal with the whole business on your behalf for a moderate fee. There are several of these in Mahón.

Hospitals

There are two hospitals in Mahón: the Civil Hospital, Cos de Gracia, 26, which has an outpatient department with a doctor on duty, and the Residencia Sanitaria, Avenida Giron.

There are also two hospitals in Ciudadela, known as the 'Hospital' and Clinica SOE respectively.

Police

The Police Station in Mahón is in San Fernando Street, and in Ciudadela in the Plaza Generalissimo.

Taxis

These are available in Mahón, in the Explanada (tel 35–1005), the Plaza España, and Plaza Miranda.

Shipping-line offices

The offices of the Trasmediterranea Line are in Calle General Goded. They run passenger and car ferry services to and from Barcelona and Palma. The frequency of these varies with the time of year.

Post and telegraph offices

In Mahón, in Calle Buen Aire (near Hannover Street).
In Ciudadela in the Plaza Generalissimo.

CHRONOLOGY OF IMPORTANT EVENTS

4000 BC	Neolithic man (pre-Talayot period)
1400 BC	Bronze Age man (Talayot period)
600 BC	Phoenician traders visit Minorca
400 BC	Greek colonists arrive
210 BC	Carthaginians invade Minorca
135 BC –AD 425	Roman occupation
AD 427	Vandal invasion
AD 533	Byzantine rule
AD 800 –1286	Period of Moorish influence and occupation
AD 1345	Minorca incorporated in Crown of Aragon
AD 1535	Barbarossa sacks Port Mahón
AD 1664	Britain obtains treaty rights for limited use of Port Mahón
1706	Philip, Bourbon King of Spain, invades and sacks Minorca (War of Spanish Succession)
1708	Britain occupies island in name of Charles III of Spain
1713	Minorca ceded to Britain under Treaty of Utrecht, legalising her occupation
1756	Minorca lost to the French. Admiral Byng shot January 1757
1763	Minorca restored to Britain at end of Seven Years War
1782	Siege of Minorca: island lost to France and Spain

1782 –98	Short period of French sovereignty
1798 –1802	Minorca reoccupied by Britain during Napoleonic Wars
1802	Britain relinquishes Minorca to Spain under Treaty of Amiens
1815 –30	Port Mahón used by American Navy as naval base
1936 –9	Minorca last part of Spain to hold out against General Franco and capitulates to him in 1939 with help of British Navy

THE BIRDS OF MINORCA

THE following 127 species were identified by an experienced ornithological party led by Dr A. R. Meetham between 19 April and 3 May 1974. The locations of the sightings are given.

ACCIPITRIDAE, eagles, vultures, hawks, etc
  Booted Eagle, nest with young at Cap de Favaritx
  Golden Eagle, near San Cristobal
  Egyptian Vulture
  Marsh Harrier
  Osprey, near Fornells
  Red Kite, widespread, at least twenty pairs
ALAUDIDAE, larks
  Short-toed Lark and *Crested Lark*, common
  Thekla Lark, a few identified
ALCEDINIDAE, kingfishers
  Hoopoe, common
ANATIDAE, geese and ducks
  Garganey, about six on Addaya inlet
  Mallard, common
  Shoveler, pair on Addaya
  Teal, party at Ses Salines salt-pans
APODIDAE
  Swifts and *Alpine Swifts*, common
ARDEIDAE, herons, etc
  Grey Heron, fairly common in marshes and bays
  Little Egret, about twelve in bays
  Night Heron, two pairs at Ses Salines and Albufera

Purple Heron, fairly common in marshes and bays
Squacco Heron, pair at Albufera

CHARADRIDAE, plovers
Kentish Plover and *Ringed Plover,* common on seashores

CICONIDAE, storks, etc
Flamingo, single at Albufera

COLUMBIDAE, pigeons and doves
Rock Pigeon, common
Turtle-Dove, common
Wood-Pigeon, scarce

CORACIIDAE
Roller, single near Es Grau

CORVIDAE, crows
Raven, common

CUCULIDAE
Cuckoo, scarce

EMBERIZIDAE, buntings
Cirl Bunting, one near Mahón
Corn Bunting, abundant
Ortolan Bunting, a few near Albufera
Reed Bunting, one near Ses Salines
Yellowhammer, one near Fornells

FALCONIDAE, falcons
Eleonora's Falcon, four near Cabo de Caballeria
Hobby, seen on three occasions
Kestrel, common
Peregrine, pair at Monte Toro

FRINGILLIDAE, finches
Chaffinch, local in pinewoods
Goldfinch, abundant
Greenfinch, local
Linnet, abundant
Serin, one near Fornells

MINORCA

HAEMATOPODIDAE, oystercatchers, etc
  Black-winged Stilt, about twelve at Addaya

HIRUNDINIDAE, swallows and martins
  Crag Martin, fairly common
  House Martin, abundant
  Red-rumped Swallow, a few near San Cristobal
  Sand Martin, a few at Addaya
  Swallow, abundant

LARIDAE, gulls and terns
  Black-headed Gull, single at Addaya inlet
  Black Tern, about twenty in Mahón Harbour
  Herring Gull, common
  Lesser Blackback, single at Cap Mola
  Little Tern, at Addaya

MOTACILLIDAE, pipits and wagtails
  Blue-headed Wagtail, pair near Cap de Favaritx
  Grey Wagtail, party of twelve east of Mahón
  Meadow Pipit, single identified
  Tawny Pipit, fairly common

MUSCICAPIDAE, flycatchers
  Collared Flycatcher, a few, on passage?
  Pied Flycatcher, abundant
  Red-breasted Flycatcher, single near Mahón, vagrant?
  Spotted Flycatcher, abundant

PARIDAE, tits
  Crested Tit, single in pinewood
  Great Tit, local in pinewoods

PHALACROCORACIDAE, cormorants
  Cormorants, a few around coast

PHASIANIDAE, gamebirds
  Red-legged Partridge, common

PICIDAE, woodpeckers
  Great Spotted Woodpecker, scarce

PLOCEIDAE, sparrows
   House Sparrow, abundant
   Tree Sparrow, local

PROCELLIRIDAE, shearwaters and petrels
   Cory's Shearwater, at sea off Fornells

RALLIDAE, rails, etc
   Coot, common at Albufera and Addaya
   Moorhen, scarce

SCOLOPACIDAE, thirteen species of wader found at Addaya
     and Fornells
   Black-tailed Godwit
   Common Sandpiper
   Curlew-Sandpiper
   Dunlin
   Green Sandpiper
   Greenshank
   Little Stint
   Redshank
   Reeve and *Ruff*
   Sanderling
   Snipe
   Stone Curlew

STURNIDAE, starlings
   Golden Oriole, near Albufera and elsewhere

SYLVIIDAE, warblers. Fourteen species identified in various
     parts of island
   Blackcap, common in woods
   Cetti's Warbler
   Dartford Warbler
   Great Reed Warbler
   Marmora's Warbler
   Melodius Warbler
   Moustached Warbler, single
   Olivaceous Warbler
   Orphean Warbler

Sardinian Warbler, abundatn
Sub-Alpine Warbler, single
White-Throat, scarce
Willow Warbler
Wood Warbler

TURDIDAE, thrushes, chats, etc
Blackbird, local in woods
Black Redstart, single near Fornells
Blue Rock Thrush, local in rocky areas
Nightingale, fairly common
Redstart, local
Robin
Stonechat, abundant
Wheatear, scarce
Whinchat, fairly common

BIBLIOGRAPHY

BOOKS

ANDERSON, R. C. (ed). *The Journals of Sir Thomas Allin 1660–1678*, vols 1–2 (Navy Records Society, 1939–40)

ARMSTRONG, J. *A History of the Island of Minorca* (1752)

BALTHARPE, J. *The Straights Voyage* (Luttrell Society reprint, 1959)

BAULES, J. *L'Illa de Menorca*, vols 1–3 (Barcelona, 1964)

BRADFORD, E. *The Mediterranean, Portrait of a Sea* (Gibraltar and London, 1971)

BROOM, T. B. *Early Mediterranean Migrations* (1959)

BRYANT, A. *The Years of Peril* (1967)

CALLENDER, G. A. R. (ed). *The Life of Admiral Sir John Leake*, vols 1–2 (Navy Records Society, 1920)

Cambridge Modern History, vol 6 (1970)

CHAMBERLIN, F. *The Balearics and Their Peoples* (1927)

CLEGHORN, G. *Observations on the Epidemical Diseases in Minorca 1744–1749* (1749); *see also* LETTSOM

CLEUGH, J. *Viva Mallorca* (1963)

CLOWES, W. L. *The Royal Navy*, vols 2–4 (1897–1903)

CORBETT, J. *England in the Mediterranean*, vols 1–2 (1917)

CULICAN, C. *The First Merchant Venturers* (1966)

DANE, C. (ed). *An Anthology of Letters: The Nelson Touch* (1942)

DANIEL, G. *Megaliths of Western Europe* (1962)

DARLINGTON, C. D. *Evolution of Man and Society* (1969)

DELAS, RAMON DE. *Stories of the Golden Farm* (Barcelona, 1973)

DELAVOYE, A. M. *Life of Thomas Graham* (1880)

EDWARDS, T. C. and RICHARDSON, B. *They Saw It Happen* (1958)

ERSKINE, D. *Augustus Hervey's Journal* (1953)

FERNANDO, CAMPS. *Breve Introducción a la Historia de Menorca* (Barcelona, 1971)

FITTER, R., HEINZEL, H. and PARLSOW, J. *The Birds of Britain and Europe* (1972)

FORTESCUE, J. W. *History of the British Army*, vols 1–2 (1899)

FURNEAUX, R. *The Seven Years War* (1973)

GARCIA, L. P. *The Balearic Islands* (Ancient Peoples and Places Series) (1972)

GRANT, M. *The Ancient Mediterranean* (1969)

GRENFELL, R. *Horatio Nelson* (1968)

HOUSTON, J. M. *The Western Mediterranean World* (1964)

HUDSON, D. *A Personal Study of Reynolds* (1958)

KNIGHT, F. *The Sea Story* (1958)

LETTSOM, J. C. *Memoirs of J. Fothergill* (including memoirs of Dr G. Cleghorn) (Edinburgh, 4th ed, 1786)

LIVERMORE, A. *A History of Spain* (1958)

LLABRES, J. *Estación Naval Norteamericano en Mahon* (Spain, 1969)

LLOYD, C. *The British Seaman* (1968)

McGUFFIE, T. H. *Gibraltar* (1965)

MAHÓN, LORD. *History of the War of the Spanish Succession* (1836)

MAINWARING, G. S. *Bibliography of British Naval History* (1929)

MARKHAM, D. R. *The Story of Majorca and Minorca* (1928)

MURRAY, M. A. *Cambridge Excavations in Minorca*, Parts 1–2 (1932, 1934)

PASARIUS, J. M. *Prehistoria de las Baleares* (Mallorca, 1968)

PERPILLOU, A. V. *Human Geography* (1965)

POLUNIN, O. *The Concise Flowers of Europe* (1972)

POPE, D. *At 12 Mr Byng Was Shot* (1962)

PRINGLE, P. *Four Fair Isles* (1961)

RAPIN, T. *The History of England* (1732)

RAWSON, G. *Nelson's Letters* (1949)

RICHMOND, CAPT H. W. (ed). Papers Relating to the Loss of Minorca in 1756 (Navy Records Society, 1911)

RUSSELL, J. *Gibraltar Besieged* (1945)

SANZ, F. *Compendio de Geografía y Historia de Menorca* (Mahón, 1908)

THOMAS, H. *The Spanish Civil War* (1961)

TREVELYAN, G. M. *England Under Queen Anne: Ramillies* (1932)

TUNSTALL, W. C. B. *The Byng Papers*, vols 1–3 (Navy Records Society, 1930–2)

VICTORY, A. *Gobierno de Sir Richard Kane en Menorca* (Mahón, 1924)

WARNER, O. *The Navy* (1968)

——. *A Portrait of Lord Nelson* (1938)

WHELPTON, E. *The Balearics* (1953)

WILLIAMS, B. *Stanhope* (1932)

WILLYAMS, COOPER. *A Voyage to the Mediterranean in His Majesty's Ship Swiftsure in 1798* (1802)

YOUNG, P. and LAWFORD, J. P. *History of the British Army* (1970)

PERIODICALS AND SCIENTIFIC PAPERS

The Annual Register, 1740–83

BISSON, JEAN. *La Tierra y el Hombre en Menorca* (1967)

CUNNINGHAM, W. *Journal of the Siege of St. Philip's Castle,* in manuscript no 6807/226, National Army Museum, London 1756

The Gentleman's Magazine, 1740–83

GILBERT, PROF E. M. 'Influences of the British Occupation on the Human Geography of Menorca', *Scottish Geographical Magazine,* 52 (Nov 1936)

La Revista de Menorca, 1969–72

WHITE, R. *Journal of a Journey to Minorca, 1751,* in manuscript no 6807/225, National Army Museum, London

ACKNOWLEDGEMENTS

I WISH to thank my family for their encouragement while writing this book, particularly my wife Tess, who helped in checking the manuscript and proofs, and my son Robert Taylor, who, in addition to acting as my agent in England during my absences in Minorca, took and processed many of the photographs and drew the general and geological maps. For the sketch of the *Myotragus* antelope I am indebted to my daughter-in-law Sandra Taylor. The photographs by Dolfo were provided by courtesy of the Mahón Office for the Promotion of Tourism, to whom grateful acknowledgement is made. The plate of Sir Richard Kane was provided by the Dean and Chapter of Westminster. Thanks are also due to A. D. Lazell for photographs. Others are acknowledged in the list of illustrations.

A brief quotation is made in the book from *Augustus Hervey's Journal* (Erskine, D.) published by William Kimber, and also from *The Straights Voyage*, published by Basil Blackwell for the Luttrell Society, to all of whom due acknowledgement is made. For the list of birds seen on the island, I am indebted to John Bell of Ramblers' Association Services, through its party leader, Dr Roger Meetham. I acknowledge the courteous help during research of the staffs of Cambridge University Library, the Bodleian Library, Oxford, the University Library and National Library of Scotland, Edinburgh, the National Army Museum, London, Linda Razzell of the Print Room of the National Maritime Museum, Greenwich, and the Secretary of Navy Records Society. In Minorca itself I am indebted to Major G. Wemyss-Swan for help from his library, and Daphne Aston,

FSCT, of the *Escuela Inglesa*, for help with translation work. Finally, I recall with gratitude the enthusiasm for my project of my late brother, Dr A. B. Taylor, CBE, DLitt, who gave me my first lessons in the technique of research, but unhappily did not live to see its fruition.

INDEX